My Handwriting Saved Me

Memoirs of a Holocaust Survivor

Albert Halm

HALM
STYLE

Published by Halm Style LLC
myhandwritingsavedme@gmail.com

ISBN-13: 978-0-6480154-0-6
ISBN-10: 0-6480154-0-8

Front cover photo: Albert, Prague 1945
Back cover photo: Albert, Sydney, circa 1998

for Roosalie

Forward

In 1992, our dad was interviewed by Steven Spielberg's *Survivors of the Shoah Foundation*,[1] and this became the catalyst for him to write his own incredible life story written so his children and successive generations could learn what he went through. The process was liberating for him. We remember him day after day sitting at his desk writing on "his typewriter" (his computer). It gave him a purpose after retirement, to share his new found enthusiasm for writing with other people and so he returned to the classroom to teach autobiographical writing, as he was exploring his own past. He successfully taught hundreds of people from all walks of life, young and old, how to write their personal stories. However, until now his own story had been neglected—so much so, that growing up we knew very little of his own personal story. It wasn't until after his death in 2013, at the instigation of our mum Ruth, that we decided to tackle the task of editing his writing and publishing his book.

Our dad had such a positive impact on so many people and achieved so much in his lifetime, despite huge obstacles. With no formal training in teaching he spent a major part of his life as a teacher and mentor in both diagnostic radiography and creative writing. He wrote 50 research papers that were published in medical journals around the world. He

---

1   In 1994, Steven Spielberg founded the USC Shoah Foundation Institute for Visual History and Education, originally called the Survivors of the Shoah Visual History Foundation, a nonprofit organisation established to record testimonies in video format of survivors and other witnesses of the Shoah. Between 1994 and 1999, the Foundation conducted nearly 52,000 interviews in 56 countries and in 32 languages.

lectured at The Sydney Technical College for 25 years and shaped the careers of almost a thousand radiography students. His most cherished moment came in 1983 when he received the Order of Australia Medal for services to medicine.

Our observation of him while growing up was of a man who was passionate about what he believed in and was never one to stand still and be complacent whether it be his political and religious views, or in his career. He was a humanitarian first and foremost, always looking out for the underdog. Many times we witnessed him helping someone less fortunate. He became the legal guardian of an orphan in a psychiatric hospital, he trained and employed a blind man to work with him, and arranged scholarships for promising Indiginous Australian students. He had such compassion for everything living, for example, he was that person who wouldn't kill a spider that ventured into the house. He would trap it in a jar and release it outside.

Despite being our mentor on so many levels it didn't go unnoticed to us that our dad was a survivor of something very tragic. His early experiences created a passionate human being who strived to do so much good for other people. Yet his family saw the scars of this experience Dad was not very trusting of people and extremely guarded. When he felt comfortable with family and close friends he was an extroverted jokester. At other times he was "the strong, silent type" and you could feel his bitterness in the silence. If he didn't approve of something you could tell by his stare.

Even though he was outwardly vocal in orchestrating and founding the Australian Jewish Holocaust Survivors Association it was always about telling other peoples stories and not his own. That is why, on a personal note, this story is so special to us. Revealing his story that was so difficult for him to voice — it's a real gift.

Our father wrote his story which included events up to April, 1999.[2] It was soon after this time that he was first diagnosed with early stage Alzheimer's. This is one man's story, a man who was probably suffering the effects of Alzheimer's for a number of years during the time he spent working on this book. Despite his illness, his voice, his love and

---

2   The Afterword supplies biographical information since 1999 up until his death in 2013.

admiration for his family, his passion for the places of his childhood and his outrage at the world's injustices - shines through.

Throughout this book you will find several additions we have made to his writing: footnotes, a family tree, photographs and maps, and a timeline, following this Foreword. We hope that this will enable you to share in his story.

This book has been edited to eliminate duplication and inconsistencies, add coherence to the chronology and structure, and correct factual errors where possible. Every attempt has been made to identify and address such errors, and the Halm family apologises for any unintended errors of fact that may still be present in the text. We have used the Australian English spelling of words.

We would like to acknowledge our mother Ruth, who made a promise to Albert that she would carry forward his legacy and publish the book he painstakingly worked on for many years.

Sincere thanks to Avril Janks for her amazing editing skills in helping us turn a wordy and often repetitious manuscript into a potential best seller!

We would also like to thank our spouses Monick Halm and Robert Harrell for their love and support.

Finally, we want to thank our father Albert, for leaving us a wonderful history to enlighten his grandchildren India, Teo, Aliza and Mika.

Peter and Bonita Halm

May, 2016

Albert Halm (1925-2013)

1925   Born 10th October in Bratislava, Czechoslovakia

1926   Brought to family home in Tchorna Tisa, Czechoslovakia

1931   Started at Czech primary school in Jasina, age 6

1938   Started high school in September; all Jews expelled in November by Ukrainians

1940   Started work in Forestry Office

1944   Nazi officers moved into family home

         Transported to Mateszalka Ghetto, Hungary

         Transported to Auschwitz, Poland

1945   Transported to Mauthausen Camp, Austria

         March to Ebensee Sub-camp, Austria

         Liberated by US Army

         Arrived in Prague, Czechoslovakia

         Started work at NSMP (*Narodni Sprava Majetkovych Podstat*)

1947   Transit through Paris and Marseille, France and aboard the *SS Teti* to Haifa, Palestine

1948   Aboard the *SS Partizanka* bound for Melbourne, Australia

         Arrived in Sydney, Australia living at Jewish Welfare Society, Hunters Hill

         Syd and Billie Einfeld became guardians

         Commenced 5-year radio trades course at Petersham Technical College

         Started traineeship at Radio Centre (Edels), Kings Cross

1953   Graduated Radio Trades Course

1954   Commenced Medical Radiography at Sydney Technical College

1955   Met Ruth Denoff at Edels Electrical Shop

1956	Started work at Sydney Hospital
	Married Ruth Denoff at the Great Synagogue
1957	Graduated Medical Radiography
	Transferred to Prince of Wales Hospital
1958	Birth of son Peter
1961	Birth of daughter Bonita
1967	Won Philips-Stanford Award for excellence at Australasian Institute of Radiography
	Selected as James N. Young Memorial Orator
	Admitted as a Fellow of the Australian Institute of Radiography
1978	President of Kingsford Maroubra Hebrew Congregation (1978-1982)
1981	Attended the first World Gathering of Holocaust Survivors, in Jerusalem
1982	Founding President of the Australian Association of Jewish Holocaust Survivors
1983	Received the Order of Australia Medal for Services to Medicine
1985	International Gathering of Jewish Holocaust Survivors in Sydney
	Compiled, edited and published the book "The Gift of Life"
1990	Retired as Departmental Manager, Prince of Wales Hospital
1990	Commenced teaching autobiographical writing at Eastern Suburbs Evening College and Randwick College (1990-1996)
1992	Travel to Jasina/Tchorna Tisa, Ukraine
1997	Nelly Wald (mother) died in Beersheba, Israel
1999	Diagnosed with Alzheimer's Disease
2007	Moved into Montefiore Home, Randwick
2013	Died 2nd January, survived by wife Ruth, children Peter and Bonita, and their spouses Monick and Robert, and grandchildren India, Teo, Aliza and Mika.

Contents

Introduction

In this ancestral profile I try to delve into five generations of the Halm family, beginning with my great-great-grandfather Avrom Dovid, and my great-great-grandmother, his wife, Sure Yente. They were a pioneering couple and the first Jews who ventured out into the untamed wilderness of Tchorna Tisa[1] in the Carpathian Mountains to begin a new life. Sadly, their immediate descendants and even the later ones are no longer with us. I found that my mother was probably the last descendant on whose wealth of memories we could rely, along with various cousins and friends who have helped fill in the gaps.

We have not been able to establish with any certainty where the pioneering couple came from, or why they chose to settle where they did; suffice it to say that Tchorna Tisa in those days was hardly a place for an easy life. Pine forests covered the mountains and the valleys, and dangerous wildlife reigned supreme. However, from all accounts, my ancestors doggedly persisted in Tchorna Tisa, and eventually prospered, growing into a large extended family by the time I was born.

The vista that greeted Avrom Dovid and Sure Yente in the early 19th Century must have been breathtaking: the green Carpathian Mountains

---

1   Known today as the transliteration Chorna Tysa. Alternate names under which you can find this place are Chernaya Tisa, Chorna Tisa, Chorna Tysa, Chërnaya Tisa, Mogel'ki, Mogel'ki, Mogilki.

together with the rivers would have made a scintillating picture for a young couple on the threshold of their lives. The winters were equally enchanting. The snow covered terrain presented a sometimes deceptive picture of serene tranquility.

My great-grandma Bruche, the daughter of Avrom Dovid and Sure Yente, died at age 98; I still remember her lovely face. This autobiography contains as much of her life as my mother remembered. Now, with mother gone, the link has been broken.

My mother was the first literate member of the family, and she made sure that I also had the benefit of schooling. In terms of religious education, I learned most of my Jewish halachic[2] observances from dear grandma Bince, an illiterate lady who ran a tightly orthodox ship. She imparted to us all the religious customs that had been handed down from previous generations, and my mother acquired her devoutness in her later years.

I remember my mother's generosity to the *yeshivot*[3] in Jerusalem, and if all their promises materialise then my mother is most assuredly in *gan eden* — the Hebrew term for the Garden of Eden. As for myself, religious beliefs are not the fulcrum of my life. I have learned to have reservations about man's written laws, and prefer to judge people on their honesty and integrity above all else.

My family endured the Holocaust; my life after the Holocaust was a blessing, and Australia was the reward.

I arrived in Sydney and fortuitously landed in the Einfeld household, and the Einfeld's became my family. Thereafter I learned a trade, married Ruthie, and our two lovely children followed.

These momentous events underpin the significance of my life in Australia. I would also like to think that they helped me to put my Holocaust experiences into some sort of perspective. As a Halm descendant I carry a lot of unnecessary baggage, which is an old family tradition. My acquired Holocaust baggage must have made the life of those near and dear to me pretty nigh impossible, and for all these foibles, acqui-

---

2   Religious laws
3   Jewish institutions for the study of traditional religious texts, such as the Talmud and the Torah.

sitions and mood fluctuations I apologise to my family. Their sensitivity and forbearance have meant more to me than any treasure on earth.

On the whole, the years have been good to us and none better than Peter's marriage to Pascale and the arrival of our delightful granddaughter India Ashley. Now, we hope and pray that Bonita will find her match. I know that her Israeli grandmother always prayed for this miracle when lighting the Shabbat candles. May it eventuate in my time.[4]

My 50 years in Sydney have culminated in a few notable achievements, from which I draw a modicum of satisfaction. They are described in greater detail in the latter part of this book and concern my professional and communal attainments. All in all, I have not made a great deal of money in my chosen career, but life has been kind to me and I am indebted to my professional and communal colleagues for having made it so.

Essentially, the reason for writing this screed is to perpetuate the life and memory of my family. I know of the work that others are doing in this regard and believe that the joint efforts will more readily piece together the mosaic of our extensive family. The Nazi Holocaust was not an accident of history, but a deliberate desire to exterminate a people.

In conclusion, I express gratitude to my dear mother for her unstinting sharing of precious memories, which materially contributed to this work. Nelly Wald survived the Holocaust, moved to Israel and lived in the desert city of Beersheva. She was a good mother and a proud Israeli who passed away on 8 June 1997.

I further wish to acknowledge the co-operation received from the descendants of Yitte, Yosel and Moishe Halm who live in the USA and Israel.

To my ever devoted wife Ruthie who patiently helped with this manuscript, I express my love and appreciation, and I also thank my son

---

4   Since my father wrote this my son Teo was born in 1999 with my former wife Pascale. I remarried in 2006, and Monick and I have a daughter Aliza born in 2008. Bonita married Robert in 2003 and their son Mika was born in 2009 —Peter Halm

Peter for his collaboration in this work. Bonita, Pascale and India have earned my love for being the special people in my life.

Last, but not least, I express my gratitude to Billie and Syd Einfeld and their children, Marcus and Robyn, for having taken me into their hearts.

In a span of some 50 years one accumulates a great many friends who cannot all be mentioned, but those who touched my life with their kindness have not been forgotten.

Albert Halm

Sydney, Australia

April 1999

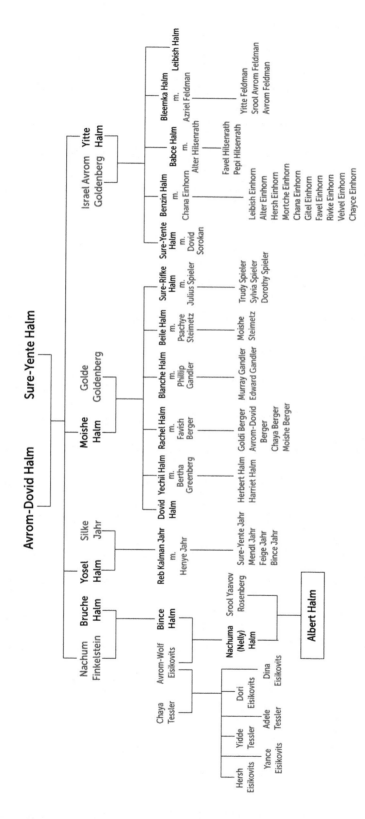

Halm Family Tree — The first Four Generations

Part I

Profile of my ancestors

Chapter 1

The Halm ancestry

As I write this fascinating story about the past I am more and more entranced by the insurmountable difficulties my ancestors endured. My first known ancestors, my great-great-grandparents Avrom-Dovid and Sure-Yente, settled in Tchorna Tisa in the Ruthenian region around 1820.

I am still puzzled as to what inspired my pioneering ancestors to choose Tchorna Tisa, setting out together to tame the wilderness in an area that belonged to the old Austro-Hungarian monarchy. Life was extremely difficult; they didn't even have a roof over their heads to begin with. There were no dwellings to speak of, and the forest spread as far as the human eye could see. They had to clear the bush for their love nest in a place where the wildlife was plentiful: the terrain was full of wolves, bears and wild pigs, all fighting each other through the night, and people seldom ventured out after dark. This austere existence just didn't seem to promise an auspicious future for a newlywed couple.

Reminiscing about the past has its problems. All my forebears have gone, and I know precious little about their lives. But my dear mother did manage to enlighten me a little. She recalled being told by her grandma Bruche how my great-great-grandparents, her parents Avrom-

Dovid and Sure-Yente, managed to cope. What she told me is shared in this book.

Avrom-Dovid and Sure-Yente had two sons, Yosel and Moishe, and two daughters, Bruche and Yitte. Bruche was my great-grandmother, and she had a daughter named Bince, who in turn had a daughter called Nachuma (Nelly). Nachuma was my mother.

My mother recalled that Sure-Yente was known as the family's rock and strength. She was a pioneer, a loving wife, and mother in the true sense of the word.

Nachuma remembered her grandmother Bruche's account of how Sure-Yente passed away. It was a Friday night. After Sure-Yente lit the *Shabbes*[1] candles she told her girls that she felt poorly, and retired for a brief nap. Then, when the men returned from the Shabbes service, they found Sure-Yente's lifeless body on the bed.

When I think of my determined ancestors in that inhospitable environment, one thing springs to mind — utter stubbornness. I am told that most of the Halm clan has inherited that trait. I do derive some satisfaction from hearing about my ancestors' struggles in Tchorna Tisa, and admire their perseverance and determination. They would have found it far easier to just walk away from it all, but they didn't. They stayed.

From all accounts they had a hard time, but they eventually cleared the land, and built a little house for themselves. The dwelling did not have a ceiling or floors, and there were no stoves, so the open fire often filled the house with smoke; but they were obviously not deterred. The house and stable they built stood there for 90 years before falling apart. None of it was palatial — it was rather primal and primitive — but their tenacity must be admired.

From all accounts, too, they stuck to their Jewish religion and pursued their orthodoxy quite relentlessly. One may well ask how they managed to get a *minyon*[2] in this desolate area. Alas, this query will have to

---

1   The Ashkenazi or European pronounciation of Shabbat, the Jewish Sabbath.

2   In the Jewish religion, in order to pray together as a congregation, ten men aged 13 years and older are required.

remain unanswered, because all of my ancestors have gone to a better place.

My Great-Grandmother Bruche's brother and sister-in-law Moishe and Golde Halm with their seven children and cousin Feige Jahr in 1914.
Top row (l-r): Yechil (Jack), Bince, Sure-Rifka (Sarah-Regina), Beile, Rachel, Feige Jahr, Bleema (Blanche). Bottom row: Golde, Dovid & Moishe.

Chapter 2

My family's country

C onfusingly, Tchorna Tisa is the name of the mountainous
district, the town and the river (the Black Tisa) which flowed
through it. The surrounding areas of the town of Tchorna Tisa
were sparsely populated, but the pine forests and the Tchorna Tisa
River made it an attractive place.

Tchorna Tisa is only six kilometres upstream from the town of Jasina[3].
During the time I lived there, Jasina and Tchorna Tisa were part of
Czechoslovakia adjacent to the Polish border. The Czech authorities
drew no distinctions between the different ethnicities in the region
known as Subcarpathia or Carpathian Ruthenia. Hutsuls, Rusyns, Jews
and Hungarians were all known as Ruthenians. After 1945 the whole
region became part of Ukraine.

During my ancestors' early days in the area, the village of Korosmezo,
as Jasina was known prior to 1920, already had a trading centre and a
sprinkling of Jewish life. Between Korosmezo and the town of Tchorna Tisa, the wildlife ruled supreme. Imagine the life in the early 1820s,

---

3   Jasina was part of Czechoslovakia from 1920-1938 in Podkarpatská Rus (Sub-
Carpathia). From 11th Century to 1920 and also briefly from 1938-1944 it was part of the
Kingdom of Hungary with the name of Korosmezo in Máramaros megye (county). It
became part of the Ukrainian Soviet Socialist Republic (1945-1991) with the name of Yasinya
and since 1991, known as Yasinya, in the Rakhovsky (Rakhovs'kyy) rayon (district) of
Zakarpats'ka oblast (county) of Ukraine. Wikipedia

before the road was built and the bridges were constructed. The waters would have flowed through farmland and inundated all in their path; Tchorna Tisa would have been isolated from Korosmezo for weeks on end. The distant farm houses would have had to be self-sufficient, and coped during the transition between the winters and summers. They had to manage; there was no alternative. The surrounding forests were carefully nurtured to provide logs. These forests actually provided a handsome income to our Ruthenian[4] population.

Both the Tchorna Tisa and the Douzhena River which flowed into it had their origins somewhere high in the mountains. They each meandered lazily down the steep embankments and formed beautiful waterfalls and gorges, giving sustenance to a great many living things. Birdlife was plentiful, and the glorious tunes woke us to a new dawn, with the mighty pines swaying in the gentle breeze. Even the waters cascading over the boulders produced gentle, relaxing sounds.

When the snows melted in the mountains or the downpours came, the rivers' size increased and the lowlands surrounding it were saturated. Ours was a mountainous area, and the spring floods were generally expected. But the mid-year ones often surprised us. Even the huge reservoir gates had to be left open, to allow the waters to flow without causing too much damage. But our old-timers knew the river well and were familiar with its idiosyncrasies; they knew when to plant the crops and when to reap the benefits.

The river's furious floods spread far and wide. Certainly the first people to experience being waterlogged were the shanty dwellers living along the Douzhena river beds. They were quickly deprived of their worldly possessions, and barely alive, they began to rebuild once

---

4   The word "Ruthenia" originated as a Latin rendering of the region and people known originally as "Rus'" – the same root word as Russia. In European manuscripts dating from the 13th century, "Ruthenia" was used to describe Rus', the historical territory corresponding to modern Ukraine and Belarus, as well as western Russia. However, the geographical implications of "Ruthenia" and "Russia" began to diverge in meaning as early as the 14th century. In modern usage, "Ruthenia" refers often to an even smaller region centred on Zakarpattia Oblast (the Transcarpathian administrative region) of south-western Ukraine. It is therefore strongly associated with areas inhabited by Rusyn minorities. After 1918, the name Ruthenia became narrowed to the area south of the Carpathian mountains in the Kingdom of Hungary, named Carpathian Ruthenia and populated by Carpatho-Ruthenians, a group of East Slavic highlanders. While Galician Ruthenians considered themselves to be Ukrainians, the Carpatho-Ruthenians were the last East Slavic people that kept the ancient historic name Ruthen. Wikipedia

Map showing the Tchorna Tisa district in present day Ukraine.

more. I did feel pity for the poor river dwellers, but I also had a soft spot for the endearing Douzhena tributary and its undisputed supremacy. In any case, the dwellers along the river were philosophical about their predicament.

Apart from these minor mishaps, the people of Tchorna Tisa were reasonably neighbourly and often helped out when the rains threatened. I can still recall how they used to gather when the rains threatened; religious differences were seldom an issue. The Jews were certainly very grateful for their help, and often reciprocated.

We lived on a high embankment and the river never actually threatened us, but still the bahna was re-saturated every time it rained. So the hay from this area was only suitable for horses, and they considered it a sweet morsel. However, since we had no horses, that hay had to be disposed of in other ways.

As I reminisce about my childhood experiences, those times of long ago, I experience a touch of nostalgia. The rustic, unspoiled charm of the Carpathian mountains attracted a great many visitors eager to breathe in the fresh air, see the picturesque forests, observe the mountainous terrain, fish in the meandering rivers, and mingle with the colourful peasantry. Our atmosphere was also complemented by the spectacular fauna and flora which held the tourists spellbound.

If you were energetic enough to rise with the breaking dawn, then you would be rewarded with the unforgettable sight of grazing deer. Occasionally the mighty stags would give a display of engagement, and lock their majestic horns in jealous combat — all for the love of a deer. Mind you, the wild stags had more sense than humans, and often disengaged their acrimonious fights long before any of them came to any grief. Usually the female deer mated with the strongest of the stags to ensure the continuity of the species, but if he was exhausted then a weaker one would do the trick.

In the winter season, the skiers came from far and wide to use the slopes, and leave their imprints in the virgin snow. At that time, the rivers provided the young and old with excellent skating facilities, and most of them came to try their prowess on the ice. So, though the Carpathian winters were long and cold, the skaters and skiers had no complaints; they loved it.

All the tourists who came to Tchorna Tisa were prepared to rough it, and they carried all the necessities of life on their backs, bringing their own tents and sleeping facilities and bedding down with their pitched tents to the river banks, near the waters of the Tchorna Tisa.

When it rained, the tourists got drenched, and the low-lying areas were also flooded. The river was unpredictable — peaceful and enchanting one minute and roaring ferociously the next — but all this was half the fun, and when the tourists got soaked during the night, they just borrowed some clothes next day. Ah, life in Tchorna Tisa was like that — unpredictable, but enjoyable just the same.

The waters held an abundance of carp but fishing in the river was prohibited without a licence. Nevertheless, the tourists would get up very early in the morning and catch a few illegal carp. The ranger had only to follow the aroma of frying to make his catch of those who were infringing the rules.

I remember spotting six or seven sizeable fish under a bridge about a kilometre from our house, and for weeks I tried to devise a method of catching at least one them. Well, finally I decided to get some gunpowder, attach a wick to it and seal it all in a bottle; then all I would have to do was light the wick, and — bingo. Of course, I was far too excited to think of what was likely to happen if anyone heard the explosion. Anyway, I went ahead with my plan, and the explosion certainly stunned the fish, causing them to float downstream, belly-up.

Excited, I gathered up the catch, and vanished before any inquisitive eyes could discover what I had done. Thinking about it now, I know my act was pretty cruel, but in those days I was rather proud of myself. However, had there been any trouble on the river, my righteous mother would have appropriated the fish and taken them to the authorities. My mother was like that.

Most of the bovine animals were kept high up in the *poloninas*[5], and at around ten in the morning the procession of horses would descend from the mountains, carrying wooden containers full of sour milk. It seemed that the Hutsuls[6] never consumed any fresh milk because Tchorna Tisa had no ice chests — so the sour milk had to do.

However, this didn't mean that we had to do without iced beer. So now comes the question: "If ice chests did not exist, how was the beer kept

---

5   A local name for a segment of the upper belt of the Carpathians that has a moderately hilly surface with a flat top and is covered by mountain meadows. A polonina is usually used as a summer mountain pasture. Wikipedia

6   An ethno-cultural group who for centuries have inhabited the Carpathian mountains. There are different versions for the origins of the name Hutsul. An explanation is that it comes from the Romanian word for "outlaw". Other explanations place their origins in the Slavic kochul—"wanderer", "migrant"—in reference to their semi-nomadic lifestyle. Hutsul society was traditionally based on forestry and logging, as well as cattle and sheep breeding. Wikipedia

cold?" Ah, that's another secret. You see, the pubs spent much of the winter gathering ice from the river and storing it underground so they could trade throughout the hot summer months. The beer had to be freezing cold, and the stored ice did the trick admirably.

So life in Tchorna Tisa rolled on without ice chests, refrigerators and air conditioners. Only the pub had deliveries of ice-boulders in summer, but these deliveries did not extend to private homes. One revolutionary thing I noticed in Sydney streets, after my arrival there in 1948, was the presence of enclosed horse-drawn vehicles delivering ice blocks to the suburban houses. This was a real innovation, predating the refrigerator. Now, why didn't we think of that in Czechoslovakia? In Tchorna Tisa, our meat was carefully stretched in the smoke loft, which kept away the hungry flies and worms.

Tchorna Tisa today is much the same as it was in the Nineteenth Century.

Chapter 3

Avrom-Dovid and the family's land

According to my mother's recollections, my great-great-grandfather Avrom-Dovid acquired properties in a variety of novel ways. Avrom-Dovid dealt in chrenyenka, a kind of bootlegged alcohol, which our Hutsuls adored. It was a drink with a very potent smell, and every time a drinker opened his mouth the listeners were demolished. Through his dealings Avrom-Dovid acquired land, especially when the drinkers were unable to pay their debts.

Now all of these things happened a long time ago and should be put to rest, but when I decided to write my story the activities of my forebears suddenly acquired a new and romantic charm. The malicious rumours of bootlegging in Tchorna Tisa suddenly became akin to the accounts of the liberating activities of the bushrangers in Australia. Both had criminal intent, of course, and if the perpetrators were caught the retribution would hardly have been dissimilar.

But I would like to think that Avrom-Dovid's conscience got the better of him when he donated land to the church. According to my mother's recollections, Avrom-Dovid endeared himself to the devout Hutsuls through this act. His generosity was acknowledged, and he did enjoy privileges unavailable to most of my other co-religionists.

The story goes like this. One day Avrom-Dovid, sauntering through the fields, was struck by the crowded nature of the Hutsul cemetery that adjoined his property. In those days the Hutsuls always buried their dead close to the church, and Avrom-Dovid noticed that the cemetery was filling up rapidly and there was no room for expansion.

So he decided to discuss the problem with the priest, who told him the woeful story of the inadequacy of land. Avrom-Dovid then offered to donate some land to the church. The priest was overjoyed, and assumed that my ancestor was ready to give up his Jewish religion as well. Never before to his knowledge had a Jew willingly donated precious land to the Orthodox Church without an ulterior motive. Well, Avrom-Dovid had no ulterior motive, nor did he have any designs on the Church; his was purely a spontaneous gesture, and the Church gratefully accepted his offer.

You would think that such open-ended generosity would have elevated my ancestor to at least a canonship by the church, or something resembling sainthood, but this never happened. Avrom-Dovid's gesture was merely accepted with a simple thank you, and this is how we came to share a common fence with the Russian Orthodox Church.

You may well regard this gesture as impulsive, but Avrom-Dovid was nobody's fool. Through his act of donating land to the church, few could ever accuse him of being a grabbing Jew. The Hutsuls remembered his generosity for a long while. So Avrom-Dovid was revered by the locals, and so were his four children, Bruche, Yitte, Yosel and Moishe. The family lived in harmony and reasonable tolerance.

However, the memory of this generosity faded into oblivion. None of Avrom-Dovid's descendants ever capitalised on his gesture. Great-grandma Bruche was still lionised for her father's deed, but when it came to the fourth-generation descendant of Avrom-Dovid, myself, there was no benefit left. Come to think of it, nobody even believed me that my benevolent ancestor had donated land to the church. Who in his right mind would want to have a Jew as a perpetual benefactor in a Ukrainian Church?

Each of Avrom-Dovid's children inherited a sizeable land holding from their father, but according to my mother the two brothers felt cheated; they wanted the lion's share of the inheritance.

Although the family house was primitive, it was in continuous family use for many years, and provided shelter for at least three generations of Halm descendants. My Boobe Bruche, being the eldest daughter, inherited the responsibility of caring for her ageing dad, and after he died she inherited the homestead, carried on farming the land, and continued living there for the rest of her long life.

The fact that my great-grandmother cared for her ageing father did not stop the bitterness spreading; in fact, it continued even as far as my mother's generation. It hardly mattered that the original feud between the brothers and sisters was a hundred years old; as long as there was a good reason to hate, they hated.

According to my mother's recollections, the rift between the brothers and sisters was so intense that neither Yosel nor Moishe attended their sisters' funerals, and worse still, the annoyance and the hate were perpetuated long beyond their graves. There was jealousy, envy, resentment and hate, all generated by a feeling of deprivation or dispossession. This epic feud contained all the ingredients of drama and human frailties that one finds in many sizeable families.

Had the brothers, Yosel and Moishe, survived a few years longer, they would have witnessed a tragedy that turned their family into pitiful paupers. The Holocaust dispossessed us all.

Fifty or more years have passed, and very few of the original contenders have survived; I venture to say that although we respect our ancestors, none of us has any desire to pursue their frailties. We have lost more than two-thirds of our family and have been dispossessed of all inheritance, so what is the feuding all about? I feel we now have to look ahead and let the unencumbered generations thrive. As far as I am concerned, I have no inkling of what the family feud was about, and am quite willing to forgive and forget past misdemeanours. Who can afford to perpetuate age-old grievances after the tragedy of the Holocaust?

My Great-Grandmother Bruche's brother Yosel Halm (left), Feige Jahr, Kalman Jahr, unknown*, Henye Jahr, Mendl Jahr, unknown*. (1920)
*Sure-Yente or Bince Jahr

Chapter 4

Boobe Bince's troubles

My dear mother was the source of this valuable information in this chapter about Bruche's daughter, my grandmother Boobe Bince. She patiently related the story to me, making sure that none of the details got lost in the telling.

My great-grandma Boobe Bruche was illiterate in the literary sense: she could neither read nor write, in any language, but she was as bright as a button in her dealings with people. From the information I gleaned, she was married twice: first to a Nachum Finkelstein, and then to someone called Hersh Chaim (his last name escapes me). It seems that great-grandma Bruche was barely sixteen when her parents married her off to Nachum. The newlyweds appeared to hit it off quite well at the beginning, and they produced two lovely daughters. However, only one of them survived.

The surviving daughter, my grandmother Bince, was a beautiful girl, but there was an unhappy sequel to this. As often happens, my great-grandma was still a young girl when she married Nachum, and he wanted to be the boss of his household, but the in-laws frustrated his ambitions. It appears that Nachum felt intimidated by the Halm family, and Bruche's attachment to the family grated on his nerves. So he asked her to leave her family behind, and settle with him in another town together with their little daughter Bince. But Bruche knew her onions, and refused. It seems she had promised her mother, Sure-

Yente, that Avrom-Dovid would be looked after in his old age, and this was an iron-clad undertaking. Bruche was the eldest daughter in the family, and simply would not desert her ailing father.

Nachum, on the other contrary, owed no loyalty to his father-in-law, and the couple soon separated. I don't know whether Nachum was of Polish extraction; be that as it may, he settled in the town of Nadvirna,[7] 32 kilometres northeast of the Carpathian Mountains across the Polish border. There he hitched up with another Jewish maiden, and had children with her.

For a good while, nobody was able to find out where Nachum was. But Nachum remembered his daughter Bince in Tchorna Tisa all right.

Bince blossomed into a beautiful young lady, and everything seemed promising. Then one afternoon her father Nachum appeared on the scene just as she was making her way home from school. He told her that he was her estranged father, and kidnapped her without ado, absconding with her to Poland. He did this not because he loved her, but because his second wife needed a servant girl. And he had one, made to measure, in Bince.

When Bince did not return home that day, my great-grandmother Bruche suspected the worst. She combed the streets, questioning every household along the way, and growing distraught when her search came to nothing.

She was devastated. Though kidnapping by a parent was not considered a crime, this didn't pacify her. In the meantime, Bince became a housemaid to her father's children in Nadvirna. She was also made to work in the local pub at night.

Bruche continued to grieve for her daughter, and then she had a vision: It was her mother, who told her to go to Nadvirna and reclaim Bince. Once the town of Nadvirna was mentioned, Bruche realised that

---

7   Nadvirna, also referred to as Nadwórna was Polish city with a large Jewish population. It is now located in Ivano-Frankivsk Oblast in western Ukraine. Wikipedia

her husband had kidnapped Bince, and wasted no time in making her travel arrangements.

A driver with a horse and a sleigh were commissioned, and they set off in the middle of the night for the Polish border. It was a freezing winter's night, but there was no time to lose. Bruche was determined to reclaim her daughter, and as they headed for Nadvirna she ignored all the border formalities. She was on a mission, with the moon her co-conspirator.

When they arrived in Nadvirna, frozen to the core, the pubs were still open, and Bruche made some enquiries; she discovered in one of the pubs that the proprietor was Jewish, so they spoke mamelooshen, the language Jews understood best at that time. Bruche discovered that her daughter Bince was working in that very pub, washing dishes in the kitchen below.

Bruche quickly descended the stairs, and soon mother and daughter were reunited. They fell into each other's arms, but after all the tears and embraces there was little time left for socialising. Bince told her mother that she had escaped from her father's clutches, and was now saving up to attempt the return journey to Tchorna Tisa. Bruche confided in the publican and after some friendly arm twisting, secured her daughter's release. It was lucky that the pub owner was an understanding man. He allowed Boobe Bruche to kidnap her daughter.

Now they had no time to lose, and began planning a clandestine return journey before daybreak could reveal the departure of the fugitives. Bince was quickly placed under a stack of branches in the sleigh, as there was no time to waste.

My Boobe Bince lay under the branches, motionless, for a considerable time. She remained there during the border crossing, but by the time they got home my grandmother was in a parlous state. She was frozen to the core, and barely breathing. According to my mother, Boobe Bince's face was blue, and the bridge of her nose had caved in, disfiguring her lovely facial features.

The repercussion of this episode was that the bridge of her nose collapsed. With this, the beauty she had once enjoyed seemed to vanish.

For the rest of her life she had a deformed nose, and the consequences were indescribable. She had cerebral fluid oozing out, and no soothsayer was ever able to help.

Boobe Bruche was beside herself; naturally, she felt responsible for the tragedy. She tried all sorts of remedies, but none arrested the flow. Then one day a Ruthenian old-timer passed through Tchorna Tisa, saying that he had a cure.

So he was invited into the house, and treated like a long-lost friend by his hosts. His face was lined and old, but he seemed to have an innate charm, an honesty, about him. "Was he an angel from heaven?" people asked.

"Tell us more," insisted my great-grandma, while watering his insatiable channels with tumblers of chrenyenka.

By this time the word had spread, and family and neighbours were gathered to hear him speak. But he was a shrewd bugger. He imparted the information very grudgingly, as if he had done this many times before.

The tumblers kept flowing and the old-timer dozed off, but his inebriated wisdom kept coming, though haltingly.

To steady our visitor, it was suggested that he be given a hearty breakfast. Now, he looked like a man who had not tasted a cooked meal in days, so the women got busy and prepared a royal feast for him. He tucked in without any hesitation, and washed it all down with more chrenyenka, but the drink didn't loosen his tongue; the cure was still deep in the recesses of his mind.

Well, according to my mother, our soothsayer did not divulge another word, and after breakfast he promptly went to sleep. Then, when he awoke from his inebriated slumber and realised the extent of the hospitality, he was in no great hurry to go. So he was given another meal and a few more tumblers of chrenyenka, but the secret cure still remained locked in his mind.

Of course the large gathering was illiterate, and the stranger's pearls of wisdom had to be memorised. The gathering was quite sizeable, but because the retention of each listener wasn't overly good, only snippets were memorised. Another problem was that a great many of those present didn't speak Ruthenian. So the accuracy of the message was rather blurred; there were also subtle nuances that people interpreted differently.

The method for preparing the medication for my grandmother was imparted by word of mouth. The life of a human depended on its accuracy; however, there were dangers other than poor memorization, which further exacerbated the situation with the suggested remedy. You see, the old timer was now completely sozzled, and the recipe he gave varied with every sentence — but then, this is how things were done in the olden times.

Anyway, his tongue eventually loosened and the pertinent information flowed freely. According to him, this was a foolproof remedy, which apparently grew in the wild; the roots alone would provide the cure. He called this weed Tshinobra, and instructed those present to scrub the roots thoroughly, then dry them, and finally pulverise them. The powder should then be mixed with grounded tobacco and smoked like a cigarette; the inhaled smoke should be allowed to permeate the nasal cavities and fill the frontal sinuses. According to the old-timer, the cure was in the smoke, not in the ingredients — it was the smoke that would contract the damaged tissues and allow the healing to occur. Well, all this made perfect sense when I heard about it, being a diagnostic radiographer. I was most grateful to my mother for her recollections, and received this remedy as a priceless heirloom.

How had this old-timer procured the knowledge? Ah, this was another secret that he never divulged. Essentially, most of those who had sought his advice knew that one should never look a gift horse in the mouth.

This story seemed perfectly sensible and most reassuring, but the question was where one would find the Tshinobra weed. The stranger had described the weed quite accurately, so the family members began spreading out in all directions to find it. They combed the hills and the dales, inspecting every bloom and analysing every flower, but the Tshinobra plant still remained hidden. Finally, they found a sizeable area where the precious weed grew in abundance, and the digging began.

They all returned home loaded up with roots, and a great many stories to boot.

Soon the roots were carefully scrubbed and put out to dry. Then, once the roots were shrivelled up, they were pulverised, mixed with tobacco, and given to grandma to smoke. Soon her nasal passages narrowed and the cranial fluid discharges dried up. It so happened that in Tchorna Tisa many women smoked pipes habitually, doing so to try to augment other deprivations. Thanks to the cure, Grandma Bince had now developed a new habit.

My Boobe Bruche interpreted this turn of events with a philosophical twist: "*S'is Beshert*," she said—it was meant to be. This puzzling Hebrew expression defies all logical explanations.

Eventually Boobe Bince recovered, but the price of her recovery was hardly pleasant. For the rest of her life she had a collapsed nose and persistent, paralysing headaches, which made life unbearable, as well as dizzy spells and nocturnal cramps. Grandma's nose remained collapsed for the rest of her life. Alas, the face that could have launched a thousand ships was now rather ordinary.

Had great-grandma been less impulsive, they could have waited till the frosts subsided before planning the great escape. But then, one is always wiser after the event.

As far as my grandma's ailments were concerned, the nocturnal cramps were the most punishing. I remember them particularly well, because she always kept an old plate under the bed to alleviate them. She used to stand on that plate when the cramps became unbearable, and soon the discomfort would disappear. The workings of all this remains a mystery to me, but if cramps are minute electrical impulses, then standing on a conducting plate was, I thought, the right thing to do.

However, I subsequently acquired more electrical knowledge, and this told me that an iron plate on a wooden floor — a metre above ground level — defies all methods of conductivity. But electrical theory is one thing, and my grandma's remedies were quite another. She knew how to get instant relief, and if the method defied the established norms — well, so be it.

In Tchorna Tisa we had the usual kinds of headaches, and something else as well that they called *kopveitig*. Now, if you think that there might not be any difference between the two maladies, just think again. Headaches are passing ailments, but *kopveitig* was chronic and everlasting. It would keep recurring tenaciously, in the same region of the head, and this is how I concluded that my grandma Bince had *kopveitig*, not the usual headaches.

So how do Jews differentiate between all these headaches and *kopveitigs*? Well, for a start, you have to be a woman to understand all these maladies.

But in Tchorna Tisa there was yet another type of headache, one that might also be classified as *kopveitig*: it came on when one encountered evil eyes. In Tchorna Tisa we had some people with continuous eyebrows, like bicycle handle-bars. These people had to be shunned or, at least, the kein nehore had to be recited, rather unobtrusively, to counteract the evil eyes. There were women in Tchorna Tisa who had to go straight to bed after they encountered those eyes.

However, I am convinced that human beings are biased, no matter how much they deny it. And this prejudicial outlook often leads to virulent anti-Semitism. In Tchorna Tisa, for instance, most Ruthenians believed that handlebars were a Jewish trait, and suspected that any child with this affliction must have Jewish parentage. On the other hand, I was told that anti-Semitism was acquired with the mother's milk.

Be that as it may, the Ruthenians no longer required the presence of handlebars in order to have a reason to accuse Jews of all sorts of crimes. I remember that when we returned to Jasina in 1992 there were no Jews about, but found the hatred had prevailed for 50 years or more. I wonder why this was so? Doesn't that speak volumes? Though perhaps one reason for this attitude was that a great many Ukrainians and Russians had acquired Jewish properties, and would not have relished the return of the Jews.

That fateful winter ride from Nadvirna to Tchorna Tisa had a lifelong effect on my grandma Bince, affecting her budding love-life as well as her health. It narrowed all her chances of a good marriage.

Apart from the collapsed nose, which altered her lovely facial features, she also suffered from a host of other ailments which would have been unattractive to young suitors. Once a girl was given a bad name in Tchorna Tisa, it stayed with her for life. So, although my Boobe Bince was as pure as the spring dew, in the eyes of the villagers she was a tainted product, and young men kept away from her.

It was a time when Jewish girls were raised for marriage, and the dowry was always a foregone conclusion. That was years ago, long before feminism ever entered the equation and tipped the old apple cart.

After the devastation of the Holocaust, there was a shortage of Jewish spinsters, so the single girls were no longer hidden from view. Many preferred their single status, and often used feminism as a cloak of respectability. In later years, Jewish girls didn't bank on marriage, and being single wasn't such an awful disgrace; sexual deprivation even suited some ladies.

Then, when it looked like she was going to be left on the shelf, Boobe Bruche even employed *shadchanim*[8]. These women, at a price, had suitors galore to offer: cripples, widowers, young men and old men. There were glowing propositions, but none of them were from young men. One shadchan claimed that she had a widower, a man more precious than rubies, who was already in love with Bince before he even clapped his eyes on her.

This suitor was a widower with five children. His wife had died in childbirth with their sixth child. The man, Avrom-Wolf Eisikovits, was a giant of a man. Since the children were minded by the former wife's parents, Avrom-Wolf was more or less a free agent.

"Now, how can you possibly question a marriage made in heaven?" asked the shadchan. The very name Avrom-Wolf Eisikovits exuded charm and elegance, and all Bince had to do was agree to the marriage. The fact that Avrom-Wolf, already a widower, was much older than Bince didn't even enter the equation; the proposition was "too good to miss."

---

8   Shadchanim is Hebrew for matchmakers. Singular shadchan

Well, Bince soon found out about the five little orphans, housed with their grandparents. The shadchan had maintained that Avrom-Wolf was as free as a bird, but in those days everybody knew everybody else's business. He was free, but only because the Tessler family of Lazeshtina[9], the former wife's parents, had rallied around when the mother died. The children were not enamoured of their father, who left them all to fend for themselves while he was looking around for another wife.

When my granny married Avrom-Wolf, she was barely 25 years of age, eleven years older than his eldest son, Yantze; but nobody knew how much older her suitor was.

All the insurmountable difficulties were soon smoothed over, and the marriage, took place in 1903, and from all accounts, seem to have had a reasonable life.

---

[9]   Ukrainian spelling Lazeshchyna

Chapter 5

Nelly's chastity

T he union of Bince and Avrom-Wolf produced one living daughter — my mother. On 29 March 1905, Boobe Bince gave birth to a lovely daughter named Nachuma, and this was when the mystery deepens. Was Nachuma named after her grandfather Nachum Finkelstein? Boobe Bruche's husband, who had deserted his wife?

Meanwhile, Avrom-Wolf remained in the old Halm household, but it was not a harmonious existence. Actually, this giant of a man spent a good deal of time away from home, working on various projects. While he was away, his daughter Nachuma, or Nelly as she was called, was growing up. Although her father was getting on in years, he still noticed her gainly proportions. The family never spoke about his philandering but, judging by the enduring hatred my mother had for her father, I gathered that something untoward happened.

Now the question is, who had the running of the house? And how much harm can a woman come to in two rooms? Did Avrom-Wolf make sexual forays at anything in a skirt, including his under-aged daughter? Well, something awful did occur in that household, but nobody spoke about it.

Suddenly Nelly moved out, and Avrom-Wolf was now persona non grata. In fact, most of the local Jewish women developed a hatred for the old philanderer, but did he violate his own daughter's chastity? That was the question nobody was willing to answer.

Contrary to all the gossip, Nelly was not actually violated by her father. However, had she remained in that household, anything could have happened. When she moved out of the household she found temporary accommodation in a friend's house. Then she managed to catch a train to Humenne, in Slovakia, and remained there for a considerable time. Barely a teenager, Nelly vowed never to return to Tchorna Tisa while her father was still alive.

On my visits to my mother in Israel many years later, I often spoke to her about the old times in Tchorna Tisa. Although it was over eighty years earlier, she still remembered all the family feuds and the countless recriminations. One aspect ever fresh in her mind was the hatred she nurtured for her father. My mother simply never forgave him, but would not elaborate on the reasons for it. This left me thinking that he must have taken advantage of her, and that even her violent behaviour towards me — her own son — had its origins in that betrayal. Her unfortunate encounters with her father in her early life had left her immensely traumatised.

Well, it is rather puzzling, the way things turned out. My mother had a further traumatic encounter. She fell in love with a man called Josef Rosenberg, but didn't know that he was already married. She was a young girl in a big town, romantically inexperienced, and falling in love was something that happened every day of the week. Most romances did not finish up with a "bun in the oven", but my mother's did! I was in there burrowing away, and she was in a strange city, separated from family and friends, with only a tenuous attachment to her grandma Bruche. From all accounts, it was actually Boobe Bruche who assisted my mother in her escape, from the *gehanim*[10] into the fire.

I am led to believe that my mother actually married this scoundrel Rosenberg, but none of the family members came to the wedding. My mother had a fiery temper, and probably didn't even invite them. I am not sure when I was conceived; was it before or after the wedding?

---

10   Hebrew for a place of punishment or destruction, used like Hell.

My birth-town was Bratislava, and I arrived in October 1925 without a hitch. But how did my mother react when she discovered that her new husband had a family in another town? The birth of a child is an eventful time; it is usually carefully planned, but in mother's case it degenerated into a messy heap! She was in hospital with baby, and my double-crossing father made a calculated retreat. Just as well he did, because my mother's fiery temper would have exploded.

I can only surmise that Josef was an exceptional Romeo; how else would he have enticed my mother to bed? In all the years, she never uttered a bad word against him. However, the upshot was that this little boy was left fatherless in a big, wide world. I still wonder whether father Josef ever gave the little bastard a thought.

Part II

Growing up in Tchorna Tisa

Chapter 6

My early years

When my mother originally left home in the early 1920s, she was a servant girl, but had the nous to improve herself. Working in the rich Humenne households she picked up a lot of useful ideas, put them in her recipe book and soon progressed to

Czech School Jasina. First Grade 1932-1933. Albert is in middle row partially obscured by girl's hair.

be employed as an "expert cook." She worked as a kosher chef in various restaurants, homes and events in Bratislava and Ushorotz.

However, she had not counted on an unwanted pregnancy. Even the rich city households of Humenne never took kindly to such appendages. So when I graduated to the bottle, my mother asked her grandmother to look after me in Tchorna Tisa. But this wasn't as easy as it sounds. You see, my mother had vowed not to return to her father Avrom-Wolf's house while he was still alive. So the handover took place at Jasina's railway station in early 1926, without my explicit approval. I was simply bundled off to the Halm family homestead in Tchorna Tisa, and don't remember any of it. It must have been done in the dead of night, when I was fast asleep.

Well, the excitement of my arrival soon died down, and the household returned to some sort of normality, but there was now another mouth to feed. Grandpa was bedridden, and the family lived on the income from the milk and butter from our cow, which wasn't much. So my mother undertook to pay for my keep, and any medical services had to look after themselves.

Our old house was taking its last, unceremonious gasp when rumours began to spread that Avrom-Wolf was making an effort to rebuild it. This plan did not go down well with his kids.

You see, since my grandpa had deserted his five children and married my grandmother Bince, leaving his orphans with the parents of his first wife, they were not overly happy. Rightly or wrongly, the kids felt that he should have looked after them rather than going off in airy-fairy fashion, building a home for another woman. Let's face it, his children were hungry and neglected, and the father was engaging in fanciful dreams. From all accounts, the children's grandparents barely managed to exist, and having five hungry mouths did stretch their resources to breaking point. I dare say that the newly built house could have also been the home of the five orphans, but it was never to be. Avrom-Wolf's kids lived on the smell of an oil rag, and received little support from him. Then, to top it all, the rumour reached them that Avrom-Wolf was arranging to float timber down the Tchorna Tisa river to start construction at number 653.

Well, apparently Yance managed to persuaded his father to let him handle the floating part of the job, and it was managed rather well. The timber never arrived, because Yance arranged for it to go to a timber yard in town, and he pocketed the proceeds. According to my mother, her eldest half-brother viewed his father's paternal betrayal with utter disgust, and felt fully justified in selling the timber. This wasn't altogether a double-cross, because Avrom-Wolf had deserted his family, and Yance was taking revenge.

It was around this time that the whole world was in a deep slump, the Great Depression, but in Tchorna Tisa it was barely felt. There our people were cushioned by a type of poverty that seldom changed.

Avrom-Wolf passed away in 1929 from smoke-damaged lungs and severe asthma, when I was barely four years old. The Eisikovits siblings also dispersed except for Yance who stayed in Jasina. Yide and Hersh went to Romania, the two sisters migrated to the USA and the proceeds of that timber sale passed into history.

Eventually my mother made her peace with her half-brother, and I often visited him on the way home from school. When I attended school and Cheder[1] in Jasina, I was often treated to hot, yummy lunches at Uncle Yance's flat. It was a stone's throw from the iron bridge, and Aunt Hermina his wife was a fabulous cook; her red paprika soups still remain vividly in my memory.

On the Lazeshtina side, about the same distance from the iron bridge, lived my cousin Yoshka, Aunt Hermina's son from a former marriage. He had one leg shorter than the other, and was a tailor by trade. I often wondered how he managed the sewing, which required pressure from both feet, but Yoshka managed, and made a good living from it. Yoshka had a heart of gold. His dear wife was always in the kitchen, but I cannot quite remember her face. Suffice it to say they were very generous and their goodness should have saved them from the Jewish Holocaust, but it didn't. Alas, they all perished in Poland.

In time my mother learned of her father's demise, and decided to return home. Well, no sooner did my mother alight from the train than she was met by her three half-brothers, all of them demanding

---

1   Hebrew school

44

a financial share for their father's headstone. This was the same father who had ruined her life, and now she was expected to pay for his
headstone? My mother exploded with rightful indignation, and the
half-brothers soon realised that it was a lost cause. They bought the
stone and paid for the inscription — and then insisted that my mother
finance its erection. Well, by this time my mother had enough, and
whenever she felt aggrieved, no force on earth would change her mind.
I bet that stone is still there, comfortably resting between the graves.

My mother really did have a very stubborn streak. And with this attitude, she disowned her father, and anybody else who might have
taken his side. I was also there to remind her of her one fallibility.
But, apart from these events, everybody in Tchorna Tisa regarded my
mother with affection; she was self educated, an accomplished chef,
worldly and inspiring company. I don't have any doubts that she slept
with men, but after her first experience she never allowed herself to
depend on them. In other words, for her men were a necessary evil, but
life could be quite pleasurable without them. Her formal education, or
rather the neglect of it, was also a persistent burden. She never went
beyond the three years of primary school, yet she had the intelligence
and the drive to do so much better.

My mother was a literate being in a sea of illiteracy. I still remember
people coming from far and wide to have her answer their correspondence for them. Mind you, her spelling left much to be desired, but she
was fluent in Hungarian, Yiddish, Ruthenian, Czech and Romanian.
Not bad for a girl with hardly any formal education.

Chapter 7

The importance of education

There was always a prevailing difficulty in Tchorna Tisa — it had to do with the attitude to literacy. It was certainly not a priority. The old timers were quite proud of the fact that they could neither read nor write, and the youngsters followed their example and to be fair, this never appeared to harm them.

Our Babushkas[2] had never gone to school, and had a novel philosophy on education. They maintained that the forests came first, and the *darabes*, the floating barges carrying wood, a close second. Signing your name on a piece of paper was hardly a priority; the three crosses were always good enough. So to our Hutsuls, ignorance was bliss, and literacy a distinct curse. Forestry work was a prerogative. While the men earned a living, the womenfolk tended the fields, and the children were left to fend for themselves.

The Czechoslovak Republic had 20 years, 1918 to 1938, to educate the Ruthenian population, and made a valiant effort at this, but to no avail. The compulsory schooling was a burden on the kids and their parents, and although they enrolled in the primary school, many never attended. Some Ruthenian kids took five years to complete the first year, and the Jewish children were no better. Even those who made it to third class were still not able to sign their names. Of course, non-attendance

---

2   Russian for grandmothers

attracted heavy penalties, so often one parent would go to jail, but the children still stayed away in droves.

Realistically speaking, the parents would have been far happier if their children had stayed at home. To them it was of infinitely more value to have the youngsters working in the fields than have them attending that silly school. There was certainly no incentive to go beyond the level of their parents or grandparents. Just as Hutsul children understood their heritage working the land, the Jewish kids were equally determined not to attend school. To them, religious orthodoxy was far more fundamental than classroom education.

However, my mother was more worldly, and put greater credence on education. So, after much deliberation, she sent me to the Czech school in Jasina. Now this school and cans of milk determined my glorious future. I remember being very anxious about going there. This school was six kilometres away, but to my mother this was a mere technicality. I always suspected that there was a motive for my going to the Czech school rather than the local Ruthenian one across the river. I could be loaded up with the dairy products that had to be delivered to the customers in town.

None of the other kids from Tchorna Tisa went to the Czech School, so I was all by myself at the age of six. I was still rather small for the return trip of 12 kilometres, in an area where the winter had to be endured for six months of the year. There were the blessed butter, cheese and milk that had to be delivered daily, and the milk cans were almost as big as I was. So, to accommodate all of these inconveniences, my schooling was delayed for 12 months. I remember being the oldest in the class, but keen as mustard to sail through primary school. But even at seven or eight, I was still small, and the milk cans barely cleared the ground when I carried them.

My school bag was always full, and the heavy cans never left my hands. Well, my education didn't suffer, and I must say that my literacy helped me to survive the extermination camps.

Just before dawn on a school day, I would be woken to prepare for school, and begin battling the mighty snow-drifts, carrying our butter, cheese and two cans of milk to sell. The only way I managed to keep on the straight-and-narrow was by following the telephone lines; they always hugged the road, except when they didn't.

Tchorna Tisa has always been a good hour's walk from Jasina and if your feet were tiny the journey took a good ninety minutes. In the summer months I made the journey in an hour, but in the winter the journey really tested my endurance.

The air was often filled with the sound of howling wolves and I was scared out of my wits. Sometimes I would bury myself in the snow thinking that if they couldn't see me they wouldn't find me. Of course they could smell me.

The road to school was either slippery as hell, or covered in heavy snow; either way, I had to drag one foot out while the other buried itself deeper in the snow. The most dangerous times were when it was dark, and the slippery parts were covered with fresh snow. Now, I could have walked on the undisturbed snow, but I couldn't lift the two heavy cans high enough. So, snow storms or not, I had to walk in the slippery grooves and risk the falls.

I still remember seeing the short sledges on the side of the road used to transport logs and the heavy loads on them; the timbers used to be secured at the front and splayed at the back. How I managed to avoid fractured bones is still a mystery to me. Because it rained often in Tchorna Tisa, the road had ditches on each side that were frozen over in the winter, and the logs just slid over them. Then in the summer, stagnant water would fill the ditches, and the frogs had a field day.

Worst of all, the silly milk cans would open up and let their contents pour out into the snowy grooves. So, while I was trying to extricate myself from this predicament, the milk was merrily careering down the street, and the packages on my back were being squashed. There was cheese in the butter; there were onion slices in the cream jars. I remember being on the ground more often than upright, but it was better when this happened at night. In the pre-dawn darkness, every time I fell, the cans of milk fell with me and spilt all over me, and my deluged home-made clothing smelt to high heaven. I would smell like an old dairy all day.

I always had to dry my clothes at the classroom fire before wearing them. When I got to school the teachers would help me unwrap the frozen *onutchy*[3] from my feet, and spread them out to dry. Mind you, the time of my arrival at school was always unpredictable, but the teachers never reproached me; I seemed to enjoy a special dispensation. They even soaked my hands in warm water, to loosen the gloves without damaging the delicate skin. Oh, they were so kind and understanding. I also recall that the helpful teachers wanted to know why I always smelled like dairy, but I couldn't tell them. That smell was ingrained in the clothes I wore, and I only had a single outfit, which my grandma had made for me.

All this happened at the beginning of my day, and I still had to face the bewildered customers waiting patiently for their dairy products that I had spilled. I explained my predicament as best I could to them, but then I still had to face my mother in the evening: the time of reckoning had to follow. Often I would return home empty-handed with no payment, and my mother didn't take kindly to this. She wanted to know where the money had gone, and I was full of excuses, but they were just simply never good enough. My mother had the wildest temper in Tchorna Tisa. It is hard to imagine that, although all this happened 65 years ago, I still come out in a cold sweat every time I think about it.

---

3   Onucha (in Ukrainian) are footwraps, rectangular pieces of cloth that are worn wrapped around the feet to avoid chafing, absorb sweat and improve the foothold. Footwraps were worn with boots before socks became widely available, and remained in use by armies in Eastern Europe up until the beginning of the 21st century. Wikipedia

Chapter 8

What's in a name?

In our family, my grandmother and my mother were named Eisikovits. My surname was Rosenberg: as I mentioned earlier, my father
was a Rosenberg, who casually married in two different cities — a
rogue of callous proportions. At the hospital I was registered as Vojtech Rosenberg, and remained as such right up to the first year of high
school.

Then Czechoslovakia disintegrated, as I describe in Chapter 26. In
1939, Hungarian anti-Semitism intensified, and since the name Rosenberg had a Slovakian ring to it, it was now highly inappropriate. My
mother went to Budapest to change all our surnames to Halm.

The Halm surname belonging to my great-great-grandfather Avrom
Dovid, he of blessed memory, who had resided in Tchorna Tisa from
the early 1800s, gave the family a modicum of certainty of tenure. The
other acquired names, Eisikovits and Rosenberg, could have been interpreted as foreign to the region, and we just could not take that risk.
In those desperate days life was extremely difficult, and most Jews explored all sorts of possibilities just to stay alive. In our case, the proven
domiciliary attachment to Tchorna Tisa extended our miserable lives a
little longer while most other Jews were already being taken away.

All this was my mother's doing, a result of her journey to Budapest in
1939 to expunge the various foreign surnames and have us resurrected

as Halm descendants, thereby ensuring some domiciliary certainty. She even managed to alter my birthplace from Bratislava to Korosmezo (the name Jasina had become under Hungarian rule) so that I wouldn't be deported.

This was all well and good, but my birthplace was still Bratislava. After all, it was the capital of Slovakia; it enjoyed "special" Nazi dispensation, like the fact that the Slovaks had got rid of their Jews three years earlier. So here was I, a Slovak by birth, a Jew to boot, and living on borrowed time.

These alterations had me all confused. I mean, for some 15 years I was Vojtech Rosenberg, attending a Czech school, and then suddenly I was Halm Bela, as Hungarians put the family name first. My various classmates still kept calling me Vojtech, but my mother advised me to keep away from them; it wasn't healthy to be called Vojtech at a time when my name was Bela.

The practice of changing names for survival purposes was not new to Jews. During a serious childhood illness, the Angel of Death had to be put off track, and so the sick child would be renamed, with names such as 'Chaim' or 'Alter'. Chaim signified life, and 'Alter' alluded to old age. So the Angel of Death would be totally befuddled, and the sick person would invariably recover, and live to a ripe old age.

In Tchorna Tisa we also had plenty of people called *Zayde* (grandfather). My dear friend Zayde, our next door neighbour, was my living proof that the system worked miracles in Tchorna Tisa. He had a childhood illness which left him quite deformed and damaged his voice box, but the name-change saved his life.

Then came the Holocaust, however. As with most of the Jews, alas, Zayde perished. He was a gifted artist and under different circumstances, would have achieved considerable fame.

Just as changing names for survival is part of Jewish tradition, so is choosing first names for offspring. In the USA there is a tradition where the son acquires the father's name and to distinguish between the two, they add Junior to the son's name. But this tradition is not followed by the Jews. In fact, it is a widespread Ashkenazi tradition to name offspring after a dead relative, to ensure family continuity.

So this tradition dictates that the first choice of the person you are named after is a parent, then an uncle or aunty, and finally, we have *Mitzveh*[4] names, being named after someone who has done your family a good deed. I had heard in the olden days Jewish names were actually traded on the open market, and often went to the highest bidder. This trading didn't augur well for the future. The children soon discovered their namesakes, and the milking began. In those days, it was traditional for a child to bear the name of a rich *balabus*, a rich man in the community, and the offspring's behaviour had to be beyond reproach.

---

4   Yiddish for good deeds as distinct from Mitzvah in Hebrew which means commandment.

Chapter 9

Our house on the prairie

My family had two pieces of land, joined by a steep, bushy section. One half of the holding was near the Chorna Tisa river and the other half was on a rise, next to the Orthodox Church. On the lower half, near the road, we grew all of life's necessities, such as onions, cabbages, beetroot, peas and beans. Then, up on the mountain, we sowed oats for Olga's consumption and potatoes for ours.

In Tchorna Tisa the small, primitive wooden dwellings were lived in until they almost fell apart. Our own old home, over 90 years old, was on the verge of disintegrating until my mother returned home to deal with it. After Avrom-Wolf's death, on 29 March 1929, my mother terminated her self-imposed exile in Bratislava and returned home. The old house was in a sorry state, so my mother decided to use her savings and have it rebuilt — pronto.

Most of the wooden houses had no floors, because saw-mills did not exist and the logs for the structure were usually shaped manually during construction. There were no stoves or ovens in the houses, and consequently the fireplace was located in the middle of the room, with the occupants huddling around it. Actually, most of the cooking and eating was also done around the fireplace, because the winter frosts were often very severe; I remember getting up in the early morning and finding the water frozen in the buckets. Most of the wooden houses had very tiny windows to keep out the chilling winds in winter.

Our own old house had no floor or ceiling, and when the winds were howling outside the smoke used to waft everywhere. So, as you can gather, our entire existence depended on the whims of nature. I still remember that smoke, and the tears flowing down my cheeks.

The timber walls of the houses were also primitive by today's standards. The seasoned timber was usually brought to the job and the shingles were actually fabricated on the premises. It was done this way because no two jobs were the same.

The wooden shingles on the roofs, manually fabricated from selected pieces of pine, often curled with the summer heat. The whole house needed attention each year before the winter set in.

We applied cow manure to the spaces between the wooden logs in our walls, to keep the warmth in and the cold out. During the summer months, the sun would dry out the manure, leaving large gaps between the timbers that had to be filled before the winter set in. So in autumn we used fresh manure for this purpose, and became immune to its smell. Actually, the task of plugging all the holes fell to the women-folk, while the men laboured in the forests.

In the late autumn, when all the farming was finished, the cows were allowed to roam to adjacent properties freely. I remember having to follow Olga around and catching her pliable manure before it hit the ground. Our impatience never made Olga do her business any faster; in fact, she often prolonged the delay. She simply did not understand the importance of her motions to our winter existence.

So in the autumn I followed her around through the fields until she did her business. Mind you, Olga never altered her stance for peeing and passing motions. It was always the same —so I would get caught in the downpour. But sometimes luck was on my side. Olga's motion would fall straight into the bucket, and I would race off home to get grandma to drop everything and attend to the task with the pliable matter at hand. My dear grandma always gave me the impression that my job was the most important one of all, and it certainly was. The holes were soon plugged, and we all slept much sounder for this.

Still, much of the seasoned old timber was good, and was reused in the new structure. I still remember how the builders allocated the important tasks to me: I had to inspect the old logs and mark the ones to be reused. Soon I became an indispensable "builder," acquiring white chalk for my task. I strutted around like a 20-year-old though I was barely six. I would traverse the mountains of timber and indelibly mark the logs for reuse. Then the builders would take these logs and manipulate them to fit the walls. In no time, the structure began taking shape, and my input was recognised at every turn. I could hardly contain my excitement. It wasn't just the new dwelling or its unique shape that promised to make it the prettiest structure in the street — it was my input and ingenuity that had made it so. I was a builder at last, at six years of age. What heights would I reach at twenty?

Since all timbers were manually prepared and fitted, houses took a long time to build. I recall that the men used a variety of honed axes and saws to fashion the logs individually. Nothing ever escaped my watchful eye and, even as young as I was, I admired the workers for taking so much care. They were very proud of the work they did, and in my judgment their pride was well founded. There was never any hint that the winds would blow down the house; the builders made sure of that.

While the new walls were rising in the house, we bedded down in the barn's loft; this was infinitely more appropriate than the smelly stable below. The only disadvantage with this arrangement was that the birds would wake us up at the crack of dawn.

We had chickens in the yard, which slept in the chicken coop. They were an imported breed — my mother had brought them back from her travels. They retired early and rose even earlier. We heard them around four a.m., when the rooster started crowing, and they carried on with the racket until feeding time. As soon as one started, all of them seemed to crow at the same time, and the sounds reverberated through the valley.

However, there was so much excitement at ground level that the inconvenience hardly mattered. Mind you, had I kept sleeping after the birds woke us, the family would have had some respite, but my incessant chattering gave them no peace. So each day's dawn brought a new look to the house, and the builders certainly enjoyed my exuberance.

Then the roof went up, and my mother chose *Eternit*[5] squares, instead of the ordinary shingles. I don't know where she acquired the idea, but ours was the only house in the district with this roof. The squares, no different to fibrous plaster, were secured on the roof, and I prayed that no stones were to be thrown to break the squares.

The house soon acquired its own beauty and character. Certainly no other dwelling in the street compared to our masterpiece, and what's more, our wooden floors made it unique. No one in Tchorna Tisa usually bothered with floors — the raw earth was good enough, despite the dirty feet this produced. It was an expense to put down floors, so the Hutsuls never bothered; only the Jewish houses had them.

Then my mother ran out of cash. The harsh winter was setting in, and we didn't have any money for doors or windows. We were still sleeping in the attic; the nights were getting increasingly colder. There was already snow in the higher reaches of the poloninas, and our new house was still not ready.

In Tchorna Tisa, the houses used double glazing and double doors. Every night I helped my grandma to stretch a few old rags over the window openings to keep the winds out. Survival in Tchorna Tisa was rapidly becoming a matter of life and death. The cold winter winds were already howling through the house, and my angelic grandma Bince, who had exclusive access to the Almighty, began pleading for a miracle.

And, believe it or not, the miracle happened. Cousin Bleema Halm (who we called Blimka) rushed over one day with the news that a Czech officer in the auxiliary police had enquired that very morning

---

5   Eternit is a brand of roofing and paneling material, made of fibres and cement.

about accommodation in the neighbourhood. Although our new house still had no doors or windows, Blimka thought that some suitable arrangements could be made with the new tenant. This made me think that there was a charitable G-d up above, after all.

A Josef Vykoukal, who was taking up a post in Tchorna Tisa, was anxious to inspect our unfinished house. The long and short of it was that he laid out the money for the doors and windows and in return, received a binding contract for three years. Then the outstanding work was commenced; in the interim, Vykoukal got hitched. He and his wife arrived at the finished house, just as the first snowflakes began falling. We primed all the windows and doors for the winter and the rest of the painting was completed in the spring.

The Vykoukals had the use of two rooms and the sunny verandah, while the rest of us were crowded into the kitchen. Come to think of it, the stove, and the oven beneath it, took up a quarter of our total habitable floorspace. My great-grandma's primitive bed, or what we called a bed, monopolised a fair section of the kitchen. It rested on four wooden pegs to the left of and right next to the cellar opening, which could not be obstructed. It had a loose layer of straw to comfort my granny, and in reality was the only piece of bedroom furniture we possessed. It wasn't painted, and it was roughly knocked together. When nightfall came, all the kitchen furniture was used to improvise the sleeping arrangements. The rest of the family slept on bedding brought together on benches that were hurriedly assembled. The only piece that was not utilised for slumber was the flat wooden table, which stood against the frozen window frame.

Then at dawn the makeshift utilities were dismantled again, to prepare the kitchen for breakfast. We sat around the old wooden table on the benches which a few minutes earlier had been our sleeping facilities.

We had a built-in container for water just above the stove; it would catch the flames and the water would boil. This provided the family with hot water right through the day and night; but, since the stove kept the water boiling, we had to keep filling it up all the time. However, this was a small price to pay for piping hot water. Thus we had a Carpathian version of the Russian *samovar*[6] right there in Tchorna Tisa.

So all these utensils were above the kitchen floor, and underneath was a vertical, rickety ladder leading down into the bowels of the earth, which we called a cellar. This cellar stored all the necessities of life — the potatoes, onions, beetroot and so on. When the cellar was opened we all got a powerful waft of potato, beetroot and cabbage, as well as the smell of dampness. Mind you, this cellar had historical significance, for it belonged to the previous house, built 90 years earlier by my ancestors.

I remember the indoor cellar well. Its walls were always damp, and the earthy odour was everywhere. It was peppered with a mixture of rotten potatoes and overripe vegetables. In spite of the fact that the cellar was under the kitchen floor, where the stove burned day and night through the winter months, the potatoes below were often affected by the frosts.

There were two other underground cellars, outdoors, also much older than our rebuilt house. Our winters were always longer and harsher than anywhere else; I remember the earth used to freeze to a depth of one metre, and consequently our cellars had to be a least two metres below ground to allow the most vulnerable things to survive. In addition, they had to have above-ground structures to accept the heavy snowfalls.

So all three of our cellars were fairly deep underground, and were protected by above-ground structures to giving the potatoes they stored a modicum of safety. But we were never really sure how safe they would be. You see, the frosts in Tchorna Tisa were always very severe, and if the potatoes got frozen, they acquired a sickly sweet taste. The cows rejoiced, and we starved.

However, Grandma Bince had it all worked out: the planting potatoes were kept in the third cellar, and they were not to be used for eating, no matter what. I recall we used to plant a half or even a quarter of a planting potato from that cellar, making sure that it always had at

---

6   Literally self-boiler in Russian is a heated metal container traditionally used to heat and boil water.

least one budding eye. Without this eye, the planting would have been wasted.

So our third cellar was always heavily protected, and never opened until springtime. The second cellar held the feeding potatoes, and was only opened when the first cellar ran out of goodies, which was around mid-winter. To venture to this cellar, we had to pick a day when the sun was shining brightly, because it stood in the middle of the yard. Each time the second cellar was opened we felt trepidation, but the potatoes never froze there.

I still remember how we used to burrow into the cellars when the sun was at its warmest, and still we couldn't be sure that the contents were going to be intact. We would remove a few buckets of potatoes and then carefully reseal the opening, so the frosts would not harm the contents.

Our snow-filled winters were very harsh and cold. The pails of water crusted in the kitchen, and even the cow's dung froze in the stable. We pampered our livestock in Tchorna Tisa, far more than they do in Australia, and certainly never abandoned them in the fields.

Throughout the winter months Olga remained indoors, chained to the wall and fed twice a day. In mid-winter we often tied blankets to keep her warm, and the stable door was also padded to keep out the hideously cold winter nights. The last job of the day was to fill all the empty containers with water so that she could have a hot breakfast in the morning made of chopped oat stems mixed with a variety of vegetables.

Our early springs and late autumns didn't suit our Olga. She was resentful when kept indoors; in winter she remained fairly tolerant, but whenever we opened the stable door, even in the middle of winter, she would strain the chain that kept her from venturing outside. Her disappointment at not being able to do so was always palpable.

As soon as spring was in the air, however, Olga would rebel. She would show her displeasure in no uncertain manner. First she would refuse her food, but then we would pamper her to persuade her to eat; she was always regarded as an intimate member of the family.

In the springtime we took Olga to visit Mrs Nedoma's bull, at her family farm near my Czech school. I was mesmerised by the size of his extended shaft. It was thin but enormous, especially, when it got near the cows receptacle. Oh, I used to have real concerns for Olga's wellbeing, but Mrs Nedoma was a wizard in bullish behaviour. While Olga was safely immobilised in a wooden fixture, Mrs Nedoma encouraged the bull to mount her and she rubbed his appendage until the bull emptied his load.

Nine months later we welcomed baby Lisa into the world. Mother and daughter cohabited splendidly together , and as it turned out , one cow was milking when the other wasn't so we had a constant supply. Although having two cows meant more work for me, we gratefully enjoyed the additional dairy products and income. As it happened before the German occupation in 1944 Grandmother sold Olga to a neighboring family and unfortunately when we were taken away we left Lisa behind never knowing her fate.

In spring my mother dug the flower beds and put up vertical strings on the outside walls, approximately 17 cm apart, to take the growing peas and beans. When beans began growing along the external walls the house became a veritable palace. The effect of the greenery was absolutely spectacular; it eventually enveloped the house and we had fresh peas and beans for much of the summer months.

Chapter 10

A world of rivers

Tchorna Tisa was the world of my childhood. The mountains, my Carpathian Mountains, were picturesque. The Tisa and the Douzhena rivers meandered lazily downstream, and the Polish border was almost within sight. Not far from our house was the Douzhena bridge, and the river beneath it joined the Tisa some 300 metres further down. Living in Tchorna Tisa for most of my first 18 years, I became quite familiar with the behaviour of the rivers.

The green pine forests stretched as far as the eye could see, giving the mountains a mysterious look, but the place was quite friendly. The Hoverla Mountain, part of the Central European system, had a snow-covered white peak, even in the middle of summer. I still remember lying in the lush grass, admiring it from a distance.

Our Tchorna Tisa river played a vital part in every aspect of our some-times depressing lives. The people of Tchorna Tisa depended on the waterway regardless of the seasons. The river water teemed with carp, and it quenched our thirst as well. Twice a week it carried the darabes, the floating barges carrying wood, and in between we frolicked in it and washed our clothes; once a year we celebrated *Tashlich*[7] by cast-

---

7   Tashlich comes from the Hebrew word meaning "to cast," referring to the intent to cast away our sins via this meaningful and ancient Jewish custom. Tashlich is usually performed on the first day of Rosh Hashanah.

ing our sins upon its waters. The Hutsuls would also stretch out their home-made linen on the river banks, and water it periodically.

The Chorna Tisa River today. Photo: Wikemedia Commons

When the river was in flood, we would catch wood for the winter. When the spring waters raged, they carried away a few of the bridges, but the standing ones were never used until they had been thoroughly inspected. This was the time when a great many households collected enough firewood to last them through the winter months.

I usually waited on the river bank with a long pole and a hooked metal contraption on it, trying to catch any stray pieces of wood that the floods might have dislodged. However, this was often a dangerous practice, because one did not know how much of the log was beneath the water: you could easily hook a massive piece of timber and be dragged into the water. I was small, so I had to pick the pieces cautiously to avoid being sucked into the massive waters.

When the water flooded in Tchorna Tisa, the boulders would disappear under the *darabes* carried by the two rivers. These enormous floating barges were made of logs, drilled and braced by four sizeable cross-pieces in front, with the trunk ends at the back — some 20 or 30 metres away — tied together with pliable strands of heavy undergrowth.

Each *darabe* had a team of two or three men. It was their awesome responsibility to deliver the *darabes* to Velky Bocskov[8], home of the sawmill, some 75 kilometres away. They used *lopatchenes*, massive oars which were returned upstream from Velky Bocskov after each trip.

Each *lopatchene* rested on a single peg, which attached the oar to the *darabes*, and the end that could be manipulated was usually at the waist of the operator. However, given half a chance, the *lopatchenes* manipulated the man on the *darabe*. If the manipulator wasn't totally relaxed, anxiety would take over, and the massive oar would have the power to throw him clean overboard. The importance of the peg can never be overestimated.

The task of navigating each *darabe* commenced as soon as its single peg was broken. One man controlled the *lopatchenes*, while the other was ready to break the peg. These men then had to anticipate every twist and turn in the river and this was where experience made all the difference. The best navigators were the ones who made split second decisions, against the formidable odds. But danger was never too far away.

The men often worked through the night to complete their tasks, but their pay hardly ever varied. They worked hard, and lived dangerously. Though used to this routine, I'm sure the excitement was still overpowering.

The flood-gates, high in the mountains, were closed off for about two days to accumulate waters while the *darabes*, still safely fastened to shore with steel cables were being assembled. With the gates securely closed, the water levels began to rise.

---

8   Velykyi Bychkiv (Ukrainian: is an urban-type settlement in Rakhiv Raion (district) of Zakarpattia Oblast (province) in western Ukraine. It is home to a large sawmill. In 1910 the village had 5955 inhabitants: 3078 Ruthenians, 1646 Hungarians and 1177 Germans by the primary language, or 3374 Greek Catholic, 1266 Roman Catholic and 1163 Jewish people by religion. It belonged to the Hungarian county of Máramaros. After World War I it belonged to Czechoslovakia, before being ceded to the Ukrainian SSR in 1945. Wikipedia

When it rained, the overflows were left open. So throughout the summer months, while the men in the river beds were assembling the mighty darabes, to make sure there was no calamity the rafts were attached to shore with heavy wire cables. This was done in case night flooding occurred.

Twice a week, every Wednesday and Saturday morning the *darabes* were sent down river. Well, most of the time a successful launch hinged on the man on the hill who had to make sure that each raft would clear all the bends before the next one was released.

If he released the first *darabe* too soon and it caught up with the head of the flood, the trouble would begin. But if he left it too late, the last few *darabes* would never leave the moorings. If he managed to get all the *darabes* away, without a hitch, he was lauded as a hero, and if some were left behind, he was the villain.

Another issue was that the *darabes* from Douzhena moved considerably slower than the ones from Tchorna Tisa, as it was a narrower river than the Tisa.

The only realistic predictions could be made by the Almighty, and the *darabes* did often emerge in the Tisa unscathed. At other times, however, it was a frightening nightmare, and when the waters subsided the grotesque pile of wreckage of splintered logs was up to ten metres high. It was hard to believe that logs 50 to 80 centimetres in diameter could break up into matchsticks, but it did happen on the Tisa.

The *darabe* workers maintained a close camaraderie, and whatever happened on the river was never carried over to the pub. Mind you, people were often incapacitated by the collisions and unable to work for months; some of the injuries refused to heal at all. But the men liked the excitement of the Tisa, and had to be philosophical about the casualties.

Most of the time, however, things went smoothly, and after Jasina the river broadened out and two or three *darabes* could float side by side. There the waters were so deep and so utterly smooth that the men often played cards or slept most of the way.

When the river was serene, we simply filled all our kitchen containers in the early morning, before the bathers contaminated the stream. Although we followed these precautions assiduously there was still plenty of sedimentation or debris at the bottom of the water containers. Consequently, it was always a household rule to allow the sedimentation to settle before drinking the water. In our household we also boiled the water in the summer, and I must say I never developed a taste for it.

The road hauliers made a handsome living from carting the timbers to the mills. In the winter, the wheels were replaced with heavy sledges, but the immobilisation of the logs was still the same: via chains and heavy tree branches. However, some men dispensed with the back sledge and the timber simply splayed dangerously, across the road, making pedestrian traffic pretty hazardous.

Summer or winter, these loads were pulled by a pair of horses. Whenever hillocks were encountered, the drivers would help each other out. Being a pedestrian, I did not appreciate the single sleighs or the sliding timbers, because they made the roads far too slippery.

Some aspects of the river brought tragedy, sadness and tears to many bereaved families. Frances Thompson summarises this rather well: "Nothing begins and nothing ends, that is not paid with moan ..."
Our lives in Tchorna Tisa had a good slice of Thompson's message, especially when the passive little waterways turned into roaring torrents, inflicting vengeance on all and sundry.

As soon the floods subsided, church service attendance improved considerably. The people would quietly inform Jesus of all the tragedies that had befallen the population. Then, the understanding priest would chant a few appropriate blessings, aerate the church with scented smoke, and send the parishioners home again. This type of treatment often rejuvenated the poor river dwellers' belief in Christ, and their belief that their plight was over. The people would return to their shanties and began rebuilding ... with God's help, of course.

The Jews as a rule didn't take up rafting or forestry work — although there were some rumours that Hersh Einhorn's uncle Leibish might have been the last Jew to meet his death on the *darabes*. The few Jews who did this work were living tucked away in the upper reaches of Tchorna Tisa. Labouring on the darabes entailed being there on Saturday morning, the one day of the week when all the Jews participated in the Synagogue services, and the Jews in my area were mostly ultra-orthodox. Even those who indulged in peripheral forestry employment, doings jobs like planting pine seedlings, never fronted up to be paid on *Shabbes* mornings; their pay packets were invariably collected by their non-Jewish colleagues.

Another situation worth mentioning is that of my uncle Yance, who worked in the forest. He used to arrive home every Saturday afternoon after work, but I wasn't allowed to watch him — he was a great embarrassment to my grandma Bince. My granny was a holy woman, and uncle Yance was anathema to the family. Yet I liked him, and when I started going to school I spent many afternoons in his abode. Actually, my cheder classes were right next door, just behind Kaminer's barber shop. Now, although I was never allowed to watch Uncle Yance drive past on Saturdays, I often sat in the stable loft and watched him rush past the house.

The land along these rivers was known as the *Zarinok*, which was always owned by the State. When our cow Olga decided that spring was in the air, there was no holding her back and I was the one responsible for her wellbeing. Consequently, I had the daily task of taking her, in the early hours of the morning, to the *Zarinok*, where most of the domestic animals grazed.

For some inexplicable reason the local municipality decided to sell portions of the common *Zarinok* to private ownership, a stupid law materialised, and large areas of the degraded pastures were quickly fenced off. Cattle were now restricted, unable to graze there any longer.

How could the Municipality do this to us? My mother was a virulent protester against this iniquity, but the fences still went up. So the land that belonged to the people suddenly became private property, and we could do nothing about it. Oh, meetings were held and protests organised, but the deed was done.

When the waters of our rivers flooded, our cow Olga would make a dash for the river, and swim in a fashion, being carried 20 or 30 yards downstream then emerging on the opposite bank, heading straight for the greener pastures. Olga was never satisfied with having to stay in the public *Zarinok*. The whole district saw her there, but Olga didn't care. She just loved a good feed.

Grazing in the forbidden pastures was a punishable offence, and when I spotted Olga in the river, I would have to rush home to pick up a rope and walk all the way to the bridge to retrieve her.

Our district forester seldom bothered to go searching for me in the bush to check whether Olga was there; he just visited the *Zarinok*, and if Olga wasn't there, the fine-ticket would be written. He never bothered to convince himself that Olga was in the bush. He had a thing going with my mother's friend, Marika; they used to frolic in the bush, but fines were never written for this. Now, I tried the same thing with Marika's daughter, who was also named Marika, but her mother wasn't pleased. In fact, she reported the incident to my mother, and I got the hiding of my life. Not fair, really.

Then the Hungarian forces occupied Carpathia, and our protests about the private ownership of the grazing lands lost their ferocity. The Jews now had far more important things to worry about; they had suddenly become an alien minority in a sea of outraged hatred.

Chapter 11

A matter of the weather

Where we lived up in the mountains, the weather changed more drastically than it did in the lower reaches. The Hoverla Mountain was covered in snow right through the summer months, and due to the cold terrain our winters lasted longer than in the other parts of Carpathia. Our cold seasons were never conducive to growing wheat or corn, and the crops mainly consisted of oats, potatoes, greenery and fruit.

The weather in Tchorna Tisa was largely ruled by the mountainous terrain with peaks over 2000 metres, and since we had no radio forecasts the people learned to read the weather patterns themselves. The majority of farmers discussed the complexities of the weather at sunset. This was the time when the next day's weather was usually predictable. Now if the day finished with clear skies then the following day's weather was going to be great. Mind you, the summer days in the mountains started off heavily overcast, and visibility was often reduced to a metre or two, but the sun would break through and then our doubts would vanish immediately.

There was a short supply of men in the scythe department, and this meant that they often had to be booked up a year ahead to cut the crops. Then all we had to do was pray for some stability in the weather — but usually the autumn harvest season was fine anyway.

Still, to ensure that no sudden change would occur, my grandma had a foolproof system that reinforced the prognostications about the weather. In the old days, religion dictated that the men had to be literate and the women had to bear the children. Though they could not write, my great-grandma and my grandma developed their own hieroglyphics, which adorned the outer wall of the house. The year's cycles were carefully mapped by my granny on the timber wall, though the hieroglyphics could never be interpreted by the likes of me. She was illiterate in the scholastic sense, but had other natural attributes which kept her in tune with nature. Together the hieroglyphics made ample sense, and often predicted the weather, even before the spring planting and autumn harvesting. From these records my grandma and great-grandma would accurately predict the weather for tilling the soil, planting the crops, cutting the grass, and gathering in the potatoes and I must say they were never wrong.

Now, between these hieroglyphics and other scribblings, the weather always turned out nice, except when it didn't. On those rare occasions when it didn't, we simply said nothing, because of all the other times, when the weather behaved itself.

In the colour-coded hieroglyphics my grandma used on the logs of our house, she would also methodically note all her borrowings, in different coloured chalks. Each colour would represent a date and an amount. The set of hieroglyphics she devised was one that only she could decipher; suffice it to say, however, that the borrowings were seldom in arrears. My grandma had a single creditor, her cousin Blimka — she was also illiterate. But there was never any disagreement over the debts. In those days, most businesses allowed credit, and the primitive accounts were kept on a wall; interest was never charged unless the borrowings were from a bank. The people to people loans relied on the inherent honesty and integrity of the borrowers. We did not have any extravagant computers to confuse the simple issues. But today every transaction is logged into a computer, and the computer never lies, so a person's word is no longer his unmitigated bond! It is rather remarkable that the computer age now dominates every aspect of our lives.

Chapter 12

Living by the seasons

We lived our simple lives by the year's seasons, which usually came around with clockwork precision. Our four seasons were important enough to our farming, but absolutely essential to the forestry industry and the planning of it.

Our springs were the balmy season; most of us had survived the winter cold, and were now looking forward to a bountiful summer. When the snow melted and the wildlife retreated, our picturesque existence was the envy of all. Spring was the time for forest renewal, with the planting of new pine trees on the denuded mountains.

So the first forestry workers would go in to gather and burn all the pine debris. Then a battalion of teenagers would invade the bush; their task was to dig the flowerbeds for the new pine saplings. All these beds had to be level, regardless of the incline, and they had to catch as much of the moisture as possible. Then finally a group of girls employed by the forestry officials would plant the saplings, in the middle of the freshly dug earth. I remember there was plenty of laughter in the mountains.

Even I worked, earning a bit of cash on these tasks. The earnings were collected from a forestry window in town, and I remember the difficulties I encountered, because I had to go to the synagogue on the days when the pay was handed out. It wasn't easy to be an observant Jew in those mountains.

Our piece of land stretched from the Tchorna Tisa river right up to the church plateau on the hill. There we planted our potatoes on one side and the oats on the other. To improve the yield, we used to regularly alternate the two halves. As soon as the ploughing was done, the oats were planted, and quickly covered before the birds could gobble up the seeds.

Meanwhile, the women were already preparing the holes for the potatoes. Then the small potatoes were thrown into the holes and covered up, while some ardent Jews said a little prayer for a bumptious season. So, while the potatoes were getting accustomed to the soil, the oats were patiently waiting for rain to germinate the seeds, but we didn't know whether to pray for one or the other. In the meantime, the mice and the birds were having a field day. Now the oats were eventually covered with soil and left to germinate, but the potatoes had to have grooves and increased soil coverage, so the women returned to do that, and the rest was left to the gracious Almighty.

Then, right across our ploughed land, the Hutsuls used to walk to church and in the process, trample over the oats and the potatoes. Now that wasn't very nice, but we had to grin and bear it — that was the penalty for having land near the Church. Every funeral procession and most weddings encroached on our planted land, but we couldn't do anything about it, and they had long forgotten that my original ancestor Avrom-Dovid Halm had donated that land to the church.

Every spring brought the Gipsies to Tchorna Tisa, to settle on the river banks. We waited for them with bated breath. The Gipsies had a happy disposition, and I often wondered how their free and easy lifestyle had become a fixture. They had colourful tents, and playful horses, anxious to be released to fend for themselves.

Their dark skins and their fine facial features have a lot to do with their Indian ancestors who migrated to Europe in the 1500s. Then for a good 500 years they wandered through Romania, Hungary, Spain, and Russia, earning a living as best they could.

The name 'Gipsy' may have originated from the English, but in Tchorna Tisa we preferred the Hungarian equivalent, *Tsigany*. Derogatory? It certainly was, but the Jews were equally denigrated, and never wanted to hurt their Gipsy brethren. When Hungary occupied Karpatolya, the Gipsies and the Jews were considered the lowest form of life. According to Ruthenian claims, the Gipsies were a cunning lot, their enterprising ways were acquired from the Jews. So our Gipsies were an oppressed minority, with a great deal in common with the bedraggled Jews.

I read somewhere that the Czech authorities made a genuine attempt to resettle the Gipsies; they even established a school in the city of Uzhorod. But the Gipsies had little experience of such residential "iniquities". The authorities even tried to coerce the kids to become educated, but this was a waste of time. Then the Czechs resorted to bribing the Gipsies, but the children still preferred the freedom of the river. So the authorities gave up on the idea, and let them frolic in the river beds as they have done for centuries.

The Gipsy children were not used to any discipline or regimentation. The authorities were equally unsuccessful with their offers of haircuts and health inoculations; the parents simply did not believe in them. If the Gipsies found schooling so objectionable, I wondered how they would react to compulsory military service. You see, our Gipsies never lived in one place long enough to acquire citizenship; they just followed the seasons. They loved this itinerant existence, and national borders never bothered them either. So, without a fixed abode, were they citizens of a district, a country or the world? I could never work it out.

We witnessed the same routine year after year. The vehicles would arrive, and form an outer circle, and the horses would be let loose while the tents were being erected in the inner sanctum. Then the fire would be lit, and a trading area designated.

In this area the Gipsies forged brass trinkets and fabricated cow-bells and sold them to the inquisitive Ruthenian population. The forging flame had plenty of oomph, and the heat was generated by a concertina contraption. With these primitive tools the Gipsies fabricated the most exquisite pieces of jewellery, selling them to eager onlookers. Mind you, there was plenty of good-natured bargaining in the process.

They also predicted the future for the Hutsul girls who wanted to know the intentions of their intended. That I could have told the girls without all the hocus-pocus, but would they have believed me? No, they preferred to hear the romantic versions from the Gipsy women. Sunday after church was usually the most appropriate time to hear this news.

The Gipsies arranged a division of labour amongst themselves. They traded horses and also worked on the roads, breaking boulders and stacking rocks; but none of these activities were ever undertaken for long. In Tchorna Tisa, we employed Gipsies to do household chores. Their chores invariably included the emptying of the toilet receptacles — a really smelly affair. If a job took longer than a day, payment was withheld until the job was completed, as our Gipsies tended to be neither punctual nor reliable. The Gipsies week usually consisted of three days of menial labour, and four days of relaxation. Permanent employment was a no-no.

Like the Jews, for many millennia the Gipsies dreamed of a Homeland. Like the Jews also, wherever they went, the people were always hostile. A good example of this similarity is that, when the Ukrainians took power in Zakarpatska Ukraina, in 1945 they called the Jews and the Gipsies "bloody parasites". Hitler incarcerated the Gipsies in the extermination camps; both the Jews and the Gipsies suffered the wrath of the swastika.

The Gipsies on the *Zarinok* harmed no one, and we did look forward to their arrival. I admired their individuality and their free spirit, and envied the fact that their children were never disciplined. Raising the young was always a communal responsibility for them, and in this was similar to the lifestyle of the *Shomer Hatzair*[9] movement of which I belonged in Czechoslovakia. However they devoted much more time to artistic pursuits, including dabbling in arts and crafts, and playing several musical instruments. I admired their violin playing and enjoyed listening to it at Jewish weddings and parties, and thought the trinkets they fabricated were attractive.

Our fairly short summers were followed by the colder autumn months, when the trees shed their leaves and lost most of their vibrancy. The

9   Hashomer Hatsair is a Socialist–Zionist, secular Jewish youth movement founded in 1913 in Galicia, Austria-Hungary. Wikipedia

only ones that didn't seem to shed their rich coating were the pines, which remained evergreen.

In autumn, the birds began congregating around the houses, and I hit on the idea of trapping some. So I carefully built a box with a little trap-door, and then put some crumbs in it and put it up between the branches in the apple tree. Ten times a day I was out there patrolling the box. Would you believe it, I trapped a little bird — the poor bird was frightened by the clatter of the lid and tried to escape. But it never made it. The bird's poor little head was crushed, and it could not be brought back to life. I was so upset that I cried for days, and never again attempted to trap birds. In fact, after this distressing experience, I made a platform in the tree and fed the birds any household crumbs I could find, and made sure that there was always water for them to drink. I hope this made up for the cruelty of the squashed head.

The autumn months always denuded the fields. All the harvesting was done, and the cows and horses were let loose in the fields. Ah, September was the happiest time of the year. Neighbours came to help each other out in the fields, and there was singing everywhere. At harvest time, people simply ignored their aching backs.

This was the season when the soil was given time to cool off and curl up and go to sleep. This was also the time when the domestic animals roamed freely and ate whatever they could find, while the owners' thoughts turned to things that needed repairing before the cold season set in. Householders inspected their wooden houses and filled the crevices with manure, or repaired rotten timbers that were likely to give way under the heavy snow. Then they turned their thoughts to firewood and began sawing, stacking the cut pieces against the closest wall to the front door.

In our house we catered for the summer, so the chopped wood had to sit in a pile in the woodshed while we suspended strings all around the front of the house to support the flourishing beans on our walls. For us, my mother's flower beds and vertical strings were far more important than the firewood for the winter. Well, I must say, during the whole of the summer we had a profusion of colour, and people from far and wide came to admire it. We had some fruit trees that looked vibrant in the summer, but in the autumn months they shed all their leaves, looking rather bare and desolate. Even the drab, faded hills were now curling up and getting ready for the long, harsh winter.

At harvest time there was a lot of flirtation between the scythe-man and the girls, but we didn't care what they did during their lunch-break as long as they were back on the job by one o'clock. The labour and the flirtations were all part and parcel of the day's work.

The cut grass was spread out to dry, and a couple of hours later it was turned. By the end of the day the hay was brought down to the stable loft.

We usually employed old Tarasyuk and his well-worn horse to deliver the hay to our house. However, on rainy days we couldn't move the hay, and we would have to spend the night guarding the grass right next door to the cemetery. Reliable sources told us that the inhabitants of the cemetery would go walkabout in the night. I, for one, believed this story, as well as any others that happened to do the rounds, because in Tchorna Tisa the dead were kept in the house for three long days before burial. I was always fearful that I might catch a glimpse of a procession of the dead. But I only ever saw the drunk vagrants who made a habit of sleeping between the graves. They certainly had no fear of any ghosts; they were too drunk to care. But we the living had ample fun and romance. I remember one night next to the graveyard bedded down between two luscious sisters and wished that I was five years older. Oh, they were such happy times.

Up in the forests the mature pine trees were carefully marked for the chop. Now, this was an involved process. Not only were the tall trees cut, but they also had to be cleaned and prepared for the long slides of timber down the hill when the snow began to fall. The pine trees were soft wood, and it could get damaged in the downhill runs. Usually two men with a saw were allocated to each tree, and once the tree was on the ground it was prepped: all the branches were cut off, and the debarking followed.

Making the long slides for the timber was also an involved procedure, because the undulating hills had to be levelled out. So monstrous timber channels were built for the pines to traverse the undulations. The channels had to be watered to make them slippery, but that was only until the snows began to fall. Then the smooth pine logs were readied for the channel runs. The wooden channel was watered at night, and an icy surface often formed to propel the massive logs through the air and down the mountain slope. To my way of thinking, the speed of travel caused more damage to the logs, but the authorities reasoned differently. So, while the logs were channelling down the mountains, the workers below played cards in heated rooms and only came out when a piece of timber obstructed the run.

Most people in the mountains were familiar with the signals given when the timber hurtled down the mountain. When *Klay-ho* resonated through the hills, it usually meant two things: either a tree was falling, or one was hurtling down the hill at enormous speed; neither eventuality augured well for any bystanders. Then *Na-Zwei-Hier* sounded, and this meant: return to what you are doing: and all the massive logs are down in the valley.

But please don't ask where this terminology came from; I haven't got a clue. However, it worked well in Tchorna Tisa. Even my great-grandma Bruche remembered it well from her childhood up till the time that she passed away at the ripe old age of ninety-eight.

By late autumn the sunsets were early, and long, freezing nights followed, which meant that winter was not too far behind. Water left in the yard already had frost on it, and the upper reaches of the mountains were snow bound. The whiteness slowly spread to the valleys below.

Chapters 13

Living with snow and ice

The winters were ferocious. We had double pane windows in Tchorna Tisa, and on very severe nights the frost made its presence felt even on the inside panes. Our large verandah was glassed in, and the Vykoukals spent most of the winter months enjoying the natural warmth there.

I remember that the snowfalls barricaded the doors and windows, and we had to burrow through to get to the stables in the morning. The outhouse often presented its own problems on cold windy days. There we had to expose our all to the elements, and by the time we were done icicles had formed on the vital parts. The cellars under the houses contained potatoes and vegetables, but when the frosts got to them the families starved. The repercussions of this disaster were felt in the spring, when there were no potatoes to plant.

The first chore on any winter's morning was to shovel a path to the river and fill the wooden buckets with water. Our farm animals were always fed first, regardless of the blistering weather.

I found the morning trips to school very perilous in the snow, when I was carrying cans of milk, butter and cheese to Jasina, not to mention my school requisites. With this load, I had absolutely no control over my movements: I was a perfect victim for the slippery snow. I also found that the horses had a similar problem; the snow was heavily impacted in their horseshoes, and their legs went every which way. And then, when inclines appeared, the horses had to try to pull their loads uphill; they found the going particularly tough. I felt sorry for the animals, but the owners simply didn't give a damn!

The freezing nights intensified, the water glazed over, and then winter was with us in earnest. The slopes were becoming more popular, and skiers were traversing the mountains in search of deeper snow.

Every change of season brought an air of excitement, and none more than the first white carpet of snow. The kids couldn't contain themselves, and some were already up there sliding on their pants, while others were honing their skills before the sun could melt away the meagre covering. Then the hot sun quickly melted the snow and ice.

We had waited very patiently for the snow, preparing for it over many weeks. One of the important tasks in the lead up to the skiing season was to trade and barter our equipment for things more exciting and precious — leather straps likely to improve the bindings, and rubber, tin and anything else that might come in handy. Even hoarding all the bits and pieces was enormous fun, especially if one could barter for or buy them cheaply in the summer and then trade them at the height of the skiing season. I remember devoting an inordinate amount of time and energy to trading belts, buckles, strings and stainless steel screws, while keeping an eye out for any curved strips of wood that might improve my downhill runs. I had discovered that clever bartering was the secret to success, though I didn't excel in this department.

All the kids were now feverishly devoting every waking minute to preparing for the exciting winter slopes, assembling their homemade skis improvised planks from beer or sauerkraut barrels . I began looking for ash-tree planks, which were much more pliable when soaked in hot water. Eventually I did get hold of some, and began shaping them, but, try as I might with soaking them in boiling water, they simply would not bend. Now what was the use of skis that refused to bend? So I soon realised that there were things I did not know about fabricating skis, and without further ado I resigned my commission.

Now I remember having an edge on the other kids in Tchorna Tisa: because of my Czech school I saw the skis the rich people used in town, and this wasn't knowledge to be brushed aside lightly.

Living in the Carpathian mountains and not being able to ski would have been a tragedy. Mind you, my planks came from an old sauerkraut barrel, and the bindings consisted of pieces of string, but that was all immaterial. The tragedy was that after each downhill run I had to repair my bindings — but that certainly wasn't an excuse to give up skiing; I simply had to keep up with the best of them.

My downhill runs were perfected even if my knees did not strictly comply with the regulations. When I arrived in Australia in 1948, I joined the N'ganagan Club[10], and we used to frequent the Kiandra slopes, but I never improved my downhill runs. My knees were somehow too far apart — a legacy from my childhood years on the short sauerkraut planks.

I was also engaged in other money-making business. This consisted of hoarding cigarette butts and selling the tobacco to the smokers; it was a living, and it cost me nothing. Another money spinner was the ten-pin bowling alley, where I returned the balls to the players and put up the skittles. None of the alley equipment was electrified in the old days, and this meant that I was always in demand. Actually, the pay per game was a pittance. With the players drunk, there was always the danger of being maimed or killed by a heavy ball, but that was the risk one took. The players seldom waited to see the skittles set upright: they had more fun seeing me run for my life. So one was never sure whether the ball was sent down to kill or simply maim the little Jew. However, once the players got sozzled,they would put all their change in a plate, and gave it to me at the end of each game.

I carefully saved this income to buy myself ski accessories, but there was never enough money to purchase the skis. I had also discovered that rust-proof screws fetched a fortune on the ski slopes, so I never used them myself; they were far too valuable. Instead, I repaired my bindings with nails and rusty screws, which frequently split the wood and had to be replaced. Talk of trials and tribulations in the Carpath-

---

10   Possibly was called Ngunnawal or Ngarigo after two local Aboriginal tribes from the Australian Alpine region – ed.

ian mountains! I remember observing, with much envy, the well-to-do skiers who simply clipped on their bindings and careered down the slopes, zigzagging from side to side as they went.

We had no ski lifts in Tchorna Tisa, and this meant that all the slopes had to be climbed regardless of the snow. If you realised that we didn't have any ski-wax either, you would soon reach the conclusion that our skiing was rather amateurish — and it was. Most of the kids in this predicament never removed their skis, because they never knew if they would be able to reassemble them again. Now, how did this compare with the skiers who carried their shining skis up the slopes and only attached them to their boots on the downhill runs? I really think we had much more fun climbing the steep slopes with our skis on and racing down on our improvised planks — don't you agree?

In Tchorna Tisa we had snowy mountains everywhere, and most of the good skiers concentrated on the mountains they knew well; those in my category were happy to hug the hillocks in town. As soon as our *melamed*[11] retired for lunch we went straight to the nearest hill to wear away the snow covering. Then, when there was no more snow, we left the hillock and went straight for the ice on the river. There again, the rich had the skates and we had the leather shoes; I wonder which of them lasted longer?

I played no summer sports, and I did not swim. You would think that with these misfortunes I would have excelled as a skater in the winter, but it was not to be; sliding along the glassy section of the river was not my forte. I invariably lost my balance and hurt some part of my body in the fall.

So I lost all interest in my skating, and began concentrating on the academic side of things, where reasoning was far more important; I was good at that. I had to excel in my scholarship, but even there I had certain trepidations, because my voice let me down: I could not keep a straight note for nuts. My end of the year results had Excellent in every subject except singing; there I always managed to get a three. However, after the Holocaust I returned to Prague and found Mr Doubrava, who had taught me in third class, and he was good enough to issue a certificate showing that I excelled in all my subjects; I was no longer a

---

11   Hebrew teacher

singing failure. Mind you, I was often puzzled as to why they couldn't delete singing from the list of legitimate subjects, until I realised that some students may very well excel in singing and remain failures in everything else.

Now in my seventies, I am happy to be alive and no longer question any of my school results. Come to think of it, I wasn't crazy about exercising either, but that I had managed to cover up. So if I list all my attributes, being tone deaf wasn't the worst of it.

I also clearly remember the nights in the winter months when we were busy making trinkets for the summer tourists; these evenings were great fun. I remember that when the Vykoukals were forced out, by the war upheavals, we still continued living in the kitchen, as if the rest of the house belonged to somebody else.

In our backyard, we had two free-standing outhouses; the newer one was the Vykoukal's and the other one, under the apple tree, was ours. But I often used to sneak into the Vykoukal's toilet because it was less putrid than ours, and if the truth be known, their toilet had a much more generous scrotal cut-out. Our toilets provided ample privacy in front, but at the back the ventilation was something else; they certainly had no privacy. Consequently, our accessories were chiming, freely, in the unencumbered breeze. In the freezing winters, one had to have a Spartan disposition to sit on the throne for any length of time. But we did have one major consolation; we could linger without ever being asphyxiated.

In our household we had a dedicated bucket in the kitchen for all our nightly activities. However, we had more potent reasons for not venturing out into the winter night. You see, the wild creatures used to roam around the yards, and they were not overly particular whether they encountered a human or an animal.

Part III

Living together

Chapter 14

Our Hutsul compatriots

Our neighbours in Tchorna Tisa were largely Hutsuls. The Hutsuls were a proud and resourceful people, often in the vanguard of their country's national aspirations. It is not widely known that in January 1919 the Hutsuls actually proclaimed the sprawling village of Jasina and Rakhiv, downstream an Independent Hutsul Republic[12]. There is actually evidence to show that a provisional parliament of 48 deputies was elected, and it even included some "misguided" Jews. Intoxicated with this unprecedented success, the bedraggled Hutsul army even marched to Solotvina, to engage the well-equipped Romanian forces over there. Well, a skirmish ensued, and the Romanians apparently chased the enemy back, all the way to Jasina.

---

12   The Hutsul Republic was a short-lived state, formed in the aftermath of World War I. The republic was declared on January 8, 1919, when original plans to unite this area with the Western Ukrainian People's Republic failed and the territory was occupied by Hungarian police. At night on January 7–8, 1919 the local population of Rakhiv rose against the Hungarian gendarme battalion, taking into custody some 500 Hungarian policemen. General Stepan Klochurak was elected prime minister of the republic. He was also active in organizing the armed forces of the republic, which consisted of nearly 1,000 soldiers[2] The army waged a brief war in the adjacent lands of Maramures. In April 1919 most of Carpathian Ruthenia joined Czechoslovakia as an autonomous territory, while its eastern most territory (Hutsul Republic) was de facto a break away state.

The state finally failed when it was occupied temporarily by Romanian troops on 11 June 1919. The territory claimed by this state became part of the First Czechoslovak Republic between in September 1919. Just for a day, a second Ukrainian state named Carpatho-Ukraine claimed here its independence but was occupied for a second time by Hungarian troops between March 1938 and autumn of 1944. At the conclusion of World War II, the region became the Carpathian Oblast of the Ukrainian Soviet Socialist Republic. Wikipedia

Hutsul traditional costume. Photos: Wikimedia Commons

This short-lived engagement spelled the end of the Hutsul reign on 11 June 1919. Then, in 1939 just for a day, again a Carpatho-Ukraine state claimed its independence, but the Hungarians quickly put an end to these fleeting aspirations.

The Hutsul households in the village were neat, decorative, and to my knowledge, uncluttered by books, writing pads and other incidentals. The Hutsuls took great pride in fabricating their own wooden eating utensils, cutlery and furniture. They never used dish cloths, and the dripping utensils were simply placed on a rack to drain. Their simple houses often had exquisite decorations outside, and covered verandahs with table and chairs — all hand-crafted.

Most of the people belonged to the Russian Orthodox Church[1] and spoke a Ruthenian dialect, heavily influenced by their Slavic surroundings. They were dedicated churchgoers, but Sunday afternoons were set aside for drinking.

The inhabitants of our village were proud to be known as Hutsuls. They wore outstandingly colourful attire as they made their way to church; their clothing featured imaginative embroidery and designs, all home grown. These Hutsul designs also had a proud, historic past, which originated in outstanding bravery.

The women were fabulously decorated in their white shifts, with colourful embroidery around the necks and puffed upper sleeves. From the waist down they wore sparkling, wire-stiffened *zapaskes* (skirt) consisting of a front and a back. The decorative *zapaskes* the women were woven with loving care, in a variety of woollen colours and featuring gold and silver braids. Their shirt sleeves were also artistically embroidered, as were their striped socks.

The men's attire was equally colourful, and they looked just as smart in their riding britches. All the men wore hats, and beautifully embroidered long-sleeved shirts over their trousers, and they also had a wide, decorative belt that was often a prized family heirloom. The sleeveless lambskin jackets were probably the most attractive of all the male garments. They featured colourful pompoms, bright sounding little bells and exquisite embroidery.

The footwear, common to both sexes, consisted of a fashioned leather slip-on with straps winding up the calves. They were called *postole*.

Most of this attire was home-made, and during the long winter months the women would embroider their outfits for the following spring. Even my mother had an embroidered white silk blouse, which she wore very becomingly over a black skirt.

---

1   According to Wikipedia, most Hutsuls today belong to the Ukrainian Greek Catholic Church and the Ukrainian Orthodox Church

The impoverished life in Tchorna Tisa was just as challenging to the Hutsuls as it was to the few Jews who lived there. We prayed to different Gods, but the results were always the same — more poverty. The only time observable relaxation descended on the populace of Tchorna Tisa was when a religious festival was in the offing. The bells would peal, and didn't stop until the church was filled with the parishioners.

During the religious festivals, it was most enchanting to observe the Hutsul families, in all their colourful refinements, making a leisurely trip to church.

The Christmas festivities were always bright, and so I decided to participate in them. My mother's female friend lent me some of her beautiful garb, and I dressed up as a gainly Hutsul girl, with make-up plastered all over my face. The only thing that divulged my masculinity was my uninhibited stride. The impersonation of a beautiful maiden went off well, and I visited the homes of our neighbours without being recognised. It was great fun.

It is worth recalling that the Hutsul women never used any leather handbags, nor did they indulge in wearing any brassieres. Consequently, the ankle-long shifts were gathered up at the waist and formed a useful pouch for all of life's important adjuncts. I must say the women had a mix of modesty, panache and a loose generosity with their sexual favours. This resulted in plenty of unwanted pregnancies, but the generous shift took care of the bulge in the early stages. At that time most girls made arrangements to deliver the babies in other towns, where their identity was unknown.

Women looked at the mammary glands as feeding accessories, rather than as sexually desirable objects. Of course, most girls hid their breasts from public gaze, and were not able to bathe in public. Since bras were a rarity in Tchorna Tisa, the bosom was often immobilised with a towel or two. How strange that, 50 odd years later, girls wear skimpy bras and two-piece swim-suits that barely cover their femininity.

The life and times of my youth were certainly different from now. I remember the married women unashamedly breast-feeding their offspring in public. In Tchorna Tisa, this was an unavoidable necessity, but how did they manage to be discreet with their awkward monthly periods? In those days, there were no pharmacies or sanitary facilities in Tchorna Tisa, yet the menstrual cycles were always handled with relative ease.

Another of life's surprises was that most women wore no panties, and peeing by the side of the road was a perfectly natural thing to do, for both sexes. So women simply hitched up their attire, spread their legs and let flow. However, this was slightly more complex in the winter, when the pee left a deep yellow aberration in the snow. But most of the time, women were daring in each other's company, and would do the task in unison. So imagine four women discussing the inclement weather, and peeing at the same time — hilarious, eh?

The Hutsul staple diet was *kulesha*, made of potatoes and maize flower, supplemented by a seasonal variety of cabbages, vegetables and fruit. Most of their households also nurtured pigs, which provided the meat content of their diet.

By and large the Hutsuls were illiterate people, but they were hardly deficient in animal psychology. They treated the animals as family members, and then, just before Christmas, the mollycoddling suddenly stopped; in the early hours of the morning, the long bladed knife appeared, and was plunged into the pig's chest, immediately terminating the loving relationship. Pig cries could be heard all over the district as these animals were mercilessly slaughtered. Pagan-like celebrations put an end to loving relationships. The loved pigs were now disappearing, and there was no remorse; there were no debilitating tears; there was no sorrow. This heartless killing was an annual ritual, pursued with relentless determination in the mountains of Tchorna Tisa. The God-fearing Jews of Tchorna Tisa never indulged in this outlandish practice. We always took our livestock to the *shochet*[2], who performed his duties of killing them for meat with a perfunctory slit of the knife.

The womenfolk would prepare the utensils for the job. The pigs took a while to die; they cried bitterly, and the Hutsuls rejoiced in their festivities. Alas, the life of the pig had but one inevitable purpose, and every last portion of the dismembered animal was eventually devoured.

---

2   A person officially certified as competent to kill cattle and poultry in the manner prescribed by Jewish law.

When the pigs' gasps ended, the women got busy cleaning the entrails; nothing was ever wasted in Tchorna Tisa. The endless bowels were washed, then stuffed with a mixture of congealed blood, onions, red paprika and other popular preparations. Even the pigs' hooves were used for exotic soups, and the pig skin was chemically treated to make the *postole*.

The bacon and the smoked meat sustained the Hutsuls for much of the year. They used to bring their food parcels to work, wrapped in cloth. Now, since their wives baked no bread, *tercsenek*[3] was eaten with the meat and the *solonina*, which was their bacon. Then, to make the meal more appetising, they would impale the bacon on a stick and hold it over a flame until it began dripping. The droplets were then directed onto the *tercsenek* and it was eaten with gusto.

Some labourers simply sliced the smoked bacon, and added ringlets of raw onion to improve the taste. When I worked with the foresters in my teens, I was the only Jew in their company, and the butt of all their jokes. One trick most of them engaged in was to slip a piece of pork into my kosher sandwiches, and spoil the week for me.

You may well ask: "How did the meat survive the summer heat?" We did not have refrigerators in Tchorna Tisa, and the pubs kept their beer cold in underground cellars, interspersed with ice from the winter rivers. The chimneys in Tchorna Tisa were primitive — non-existent, you might say. But all the households burned wood and the smoke used to rise into the lofts, where the carcasses were laid out to be preserved. So in the summer, with electricity still many years away, the meat was cured in the lofts.

The hungry meat-worms were not overly fussy, and the Hutsuls would brush off the vermin and merrily eat the meat. They even tried to share this disgusting habit with me, but I always found some lame excuse not to participate.

There was much drinking in Tchorna Tisa, and since we lived almost next door to Blimka's pub we often endured the consequences of intoxication. Mind you, the Hutsuls were tolerant towards the observant Jews, and used to line up for their evening quota on Saturday evening

---

3   Unsure of the translation for this food – ed.

after the Sabbath when the three stars appeared in heaven. Blimka's pub never opened before the lights were lit and the *Havdalla*[4] was recited. Then about an hour later, the *darabe* people would arrive from Velky Bocskov, all parched, for a frothy beer, and the celebrations would get under way. The men told hair-raising yarns about events, some of which had never happened, but their accounts were enjoyed all the same. Then, after a few friendly exchanges, the alcohol got the better of them and their tolerance began to wane. Some became belligerent, and brawls followed, with glasses being broken. But the troublemakers were quickly isolated, and they vented their anger in the street. The injuries were never serious enough to require medical attention, though there were doctors available in Tchorna Tisa anyway.

---

4   A Jewish religious ceremony that marks the symbolic end of Shabbat and Jewish holidays, and ushers in the new week. The ritual involves lighting a special havdalah candle with several wicks, blessing a cup of wine and smelling sweet spices.

Chapter 15

A Jewish way of life

O ur household was ultra-orthodox, and we observed the Jewish dietary laws strictly. We had *fleishik, milchik* and *pareve* meals[5]. Our mid-week meals consisted of either *pareve* or *milchik* dishes. But the Friday night and Shabbes goodies were always *fleishik*. The law separating *milchik* and *fleishik* was strictly observed by Jews in Tchorna Tisa, and we would never eat *milchik* food for six hours after a *fleishik* meal. However, the reverse was less strict, and after a *milchik* dish it was only three hours until we could eat a *fleishik* meal. This was a tradition, and one never disputed traditions.

It is also worth recalling that, apart from our meat dishes and associated cutlery, all our other kitchen utensils were made of wood. The reasoning behind this orthodox peculiarity was that porous dishes have the capacity to absorb *fleishik* flavours.

Now, with this in mind, did we use separate sinks for the dishes? Well, in Tchorna Tisa we didn't have sinks of any kind, so the dishes were washed in separate buckets — *fleishik, milchik* and *pareve*.

---

5   Kosher foods are divided into three categories: fleishik - meat, milchik - dairy and pareve. One of the basic principles of kosher eating is the total separation of meat and dairy products. Meat and dairy may not be cooked or eaten together. To ensure this, the kosher kitchen contains separate sets of dishes, utensils, cookware, and separate preparation areas for meat and dairy. A third category, pareve, is comprised of foods which are neither meat nor dairy and may therefore be eaten with either.

We grew no wheat in Jasina, and bread seemed a luxury, but no Jewish household ever economised on the Holy *Shabbes*. The sacred seventh day always saw a couple of plaited Challahs adorning the table, baked with store bought flour. The meal invariably consisted of hot chicken soup, and at least one meat dish. We had a poor household, and we often stinted during the week so as to ensure that the *Shabbes* meal met all the religious expectations; it was less than Jewish not to highlight the day of rest.

On Friday mornings as soon as the baking was finished, Grandma Bince had all the *Shabbes* dishes ready to go into the hot oven, and there they simmered all night. For the *Cholent*[6], the oven had to be sealed, and grandma was the expert here. She used a heavy board against the oven opening, and sealed it with fresh cow manure; this ensured that the *Shabbes* meal was going to be cooked to perfection. To the uninitiated, the word *Cholent* may conjure up something prehistoric, but in fact this was the midday meal for *Shabbes*. I don't quite know where the word *Cholent* originated, but suffice it to say it encapsulates everything that a self-respecting Jew would wish to have on his *Shabbes* table.

There are certain ingredients without which the *Cholent* would not be a *Cholent*. Principally, it must contain meat, potatoes, beans and other secret goodies that only my granny knew about. Then, the heat of the oven must be such that the *Cholent* will be cooked by next lunchtime, but not burned. When I came home from *Shule*[7] on Saturdays, grandma had the traditional dish of eggs mixed with raw onions ready, and this was followed by a steaming hot vegetable soup, after which the oven was opened to reveal the *Cholent*. Of course there was an art to all this, handed down through the generations of *Yiddishkeit*[8] . I am not even sure that I ought divulge the intimate secrets of the *Cholent*; it was steeped in history and tradition, and boiled down to the consistency of cow's manure.

---

6   Yiddish word for a traditional Jewish stew. It is usually simmered overnight for 12 hours or more, and eaten for lunch on Shabbat . The pot is brought to a boil on Friday before the Sabbath begins, and kept on a blech or hotplate, or placed in a slow oven until the following day. There are many variations of the dish. The basic ingredients of cholent are meat, potatoes, beans and barley.

7   Common name for Synagogue.

8   Literally means "Jewishness", i.e. "a Jewish way of life", in the Yiddish language.

In those days, tradition used to rule our lives, and the poor Jews never seemed to mind that they lived on the smell of an oil rag just so they could make the *Shabbes* fit for a king. Certainly, my Boobe Bince observed all the virtuous traditions, even if this brought hardship on the household. I remember thriving on the leftovers on Sundays, and then for the rest of the week subsisting on *kulesha* — mashed boiled potatoes with maize flour. Now, you have not lived till you taste *kulesha* topped with melted butter and pungent *brindse*, a type of goat cheese. This used to make a fabulous evening meal, but then the thought of having to eat the cold leftover *kulesha* with hot milk next morning quickly soured all the enjoyment. It all tasted very delicious at night, but the same *kulesha* next morning was barely edible.

My mother put it in front of me, and I can still hear her endearing words: "You either eat or perish. Which is it to be?" I ate, and there were more salty tears on the *kulesha* than hot milk. This never softened my mother. "Eat now and vomit it up later," she used to say.

We had other sets of cutlery and crockery for *Pesach*[9], the festival of Passover, and they were again divided into *fleishik, milchik* and *pareve*. The meat utensils and the separate cutlery were only used on Friday nights, and *Shabbes* lunch time. During the rest of the week, we had *milchik* and *pareve* utensils, exclusively. However, anything that was *pareve* was neutral, and could be used with either *fleishik* or *milchik* dishes.

I also remember that all our *Pesach* utensils were carefully wrapped in sheets after *Pesach*, and carried up the ladder to the loft of the house. Then they were covered again, so that no dampness would get to them, and they stayed there for the whole year. I recall my dear grandma making sure that the *Pesach* dishes were not brought down until the whole house was made *Pesachdic*[10]. This meant that the floors had to be scrubbed, the walls painted, and all the furniture wiped over for the holy days.

---

9 Commemorates the story of the Exodus as described in the Hebrew Bible in which the Israelites were freed from slavery in Egypt. A symbol of the Passover holiday is matzo, an unleavened flatbread made solely from flour and water. All leavened bread/food is forbidden for 8 days.
10 Observant Jews spend the weeks before Passover in a flurry of housecleaning, to remove every morsel of chametz (leavened food).

Prior to *Pesach*, all the ordinary dishes were put away, and the *Pesach* dishes brought down and thoroughly cleaned; this ensured that we were literally fasting the whole day. All this was done to remember our forebears in the desert of Egypt; the whole house would be turned upside down for the eight days of *Pesach*. My Boobe Bince always wished it to be so or, maybe it was the custom of the times. The *matzos* could not be touched until the prayers were said, and the prayers could not be intoned until the men returned from the Synagogue when *Pesach* began. But that wasn't the half of it; even when the men returned, our table could still not be disturbed, because before we ate we had to recall all the afflictions of our forefathers in Ancient Egypt according to the Haggadah prayer book. So my memories of our *Seder*[11] nights are largely focused on the gnawing pains in my stomach. Finally my loving grandma put the steaming hot soup on the table, and our little family rejoiced.

The Hutsuls looked on, with good natured amusement, as the Jews cleaned, polished and baked matzos for their Passover. Of course, the Hutsuls had their own food and holiday preparations, which were pursued with the same zeal, and uncompromising determination.

In the town of Jasina, the Jews were thick on the ground[12]. The bulk of the Jews lived and traded within a radius of one kilometre of the iron bridge which was the centre of the universe. But they were observant, the holidays were strictly adhered to and there was always a minyon to be had.

If you have concluded that no Jews lived beyond this radius, let me assure you that the Jews resided all over the place. However, as far as business was concerned, the Jews conducted it within this magic kilometre. Beyond this area reigned poverty and a semblance of Jewish farming, but the Jews pulled together — here was a good deal of communal cohesion.

---

11   It is traditional for Jewish families to gather on the first 2 nights of Passover for a special dinner called a seder.
12   In 1921, in Jasina there were 9401 inhabitants including 6649 Ukrainians, 1392 Jews, 678 Hungarians, 396 Germans, 165 Czechs and Slovaks and 8 Romanians. Wikipedia

Jews married Jews in Tchorna Tisa. I did hear of two Jewish women in Jasina who married Catholic men, and brought shame on their families. So their parents immediately disowned them, and sat *Shiva*[13].

Our married women used to crop their hair, and then wore kerchiefs or wigs to cover their bare heads. But how did they manage without the monthly dip in the *Mikveh*[14], which was six kilometres away?

In the region, most Jews of the Orthodox persuasion wore the familiar black kaftans, the wide-brimmed hats, and the long beards. They lived in the traditions of the Middle Ages, stringently adhering to their religion. Mind you, it wasn't easy to be a practising Jew in Tchorna Tisa: we observed, fervently, all the commandments, although we put aside those that did not suit us.

Many of our Jews refrained from being too conspicuous. For instance, I never had the traditional curly locks hanging around my ears, and nor did I wear *tzitzis*[15], or tassels that hung from my waist, because both of these appendages invited anti-Semitic outbursts and ridicule.

My uncle Yance, who wasn't overly observant, worked on *Shabbes,* in the forest, and was often seen returning home on Saturday afternoons, with his horses, but that was never spoken about. According to my granny's interpretation, if I saw him driving the horses on the Holy *Shabbes*, this would mean that I approved of his deeds.

A predicament, for us was the required circumcision of the new-born lads. We did not have a *mohel*[16] in Tchorna Tisa to do this, nor did we need a dedicated *mohel* for the few families who lived there. On the occasions when a boy materialised, the Jasina Mohel played hard to get, and who could blame him? Tchorna Tisa was out in the sticks

---

13   The week-long mourning period after a death in Judaism for first-degree relatives: father, mother, son, daughter, brother, sister, and spouse. The ritual is referred to as "sitting shiva."
14   A bath used for the purpose of ritual immersion in Judaism. A woman is required to immerse in a mikveh after her menstrual period or childbirth before she and her husband can resume marital relations. Wikipedia
15   The name for specially knotted ritual fringes, or tassels, worn in antiquity by Israelites and today by observant Jews and Samaritans. Tzitzit are attached to the four corners of the tallit (prayer shawl) and tallit katan (everyday undergarment).
16   A Jewish person trained in the practice of brit milah, the covenant of circumcision. Wikipedia

and he was handsomely remunerated in town, and to hell with us; his "chopping stakes" never extended that far.

Right up to the Holocaust, we Jews of Tchorna Tisa put our collective trust in the Almighty, and things always seemed to work out. The Jewish Messiah who kept our hopes buoyant through the ages was ignored by the Nazis. This was the same Messiah who promised to deliver us to the Promised Land. During my early years, I fervently believed in all these prophecies, and even kept a secret parcel packed for the long journey to Israel. In my reflective moments, I did speculate about the health of the elderly and the sick. How would they attempt the arduous journey to the Promised Land? Some of these people were already far too feeble to make it to the toilet, let alone cross the oceans to Jerusalem. But our journey out of Tchorna took us to Auschwitz instead of Israel.

Chapter 16

Our Jewish neighbours

If I stood in the street and faced our house, we were surrounded by relatives; the Jahr family would be living on the right-hand side and the Feldman and Einhorn families on the left. The Feldman parents were Blimka (Halm) and Azriel Feldman, and Blimka's brother Benzin (Halm) and his wife Chana Einhorn who used her surname.

My relatives Bleema and Azriel had three children: Yitte, Srool Avrom (Sruelic) and Avrom (Avromele.) They were all my playmates, but Yitte was the eldest daughter, and closest to my age, so the two of us discussed worldly things, like procreation.

Once this discussion was over, we delved into more substantial matters. I was convinced that babies were manufactured, not produced: I thought, in general, that peeing into a hole in the ground should create an offspring or two. So we took our marriage vows in the back yard, and wasted no time in digging the holes for procreation. Then we carefully peed into them, and raced there every day to observe our babies' growth. But the holes remained empty. Why was that, we wanted to know.

Then Yitte hit on the idea that the holes needed to be watered. So we watered them regularly, and only peed into the holes occasionally, but this just encouraged the grass to grow. We concluded that babies were a matter of trial and error, and it wasn't the time to procreate. So parenthood was postponed for a few years.

Although Reb Benzin was my great-grandmother's first cousin, hardly anyone knew that we were related. They lived very private lives, spoke to no one, and prayed at home. Reb Benzin had something wrong with one leg, and the kids often emulated his walk — with a generous smattering of goodwill.

However, Reb Benzin grew remarkable cabbages; they were the talk of the district. I remember people coming from far and wide to admire them, but people never raided his crop. You see, Reb Benzin had his own delectable recipe for the cabbages: he fertilised the soil with the contents of his lavatory box, and the aroma inundated the district. I can still smell the aroma even 50 odd years later; the winds used to blow it between our double doors, and every crevice smelled of lavatory. Then in due course he had these enormous cabbages, which the family consumed, but seldom would anyone else share in the spoils.

The Jahr family was headed by Reb Kalmen and his wife Henya. Reb Kalmen had all the trimmings of a devout human being; he even wore a *yarmulke*, which never left his bald patch. I remember that *yarmulke*: it was always at the back of his head, with a black hat pushed forward shading his worried brow. Now, being ultra-orthodox, Reb Kalmen also had curly *payes*, which swayed in the breeze, and the darkish beard was just a little too sparse to add dignity to his lined face. His black garb, and the *tzitzis* which also adorned his manageable midriff, gave him the outward appearance of a holy man — a *tzadik*.

There was a property dividing us from Reb Kalmen's; it belonged to our relatives the Hilsenrath family, who lived in Jasina. Reb Kalmen, of blessed memory, had a mighty quirk — and who hasn't? He liked to fiddle with the fence-posts, and his portion of the land always seemed to grow in width — to extend a few centimetres, rather than diminish, in the process. We all knew that he was in the habit of moving the wire fence. His incursions occurred with monotonous regularity, yet from all appearances he was a Holy Man. And this was where the contradiction arose — who could accuse Reb Kalmen of such a thing?

The other peculiarity of Reb Kalmen's was never to return anything he borrowed. Reb Kalmen believed in unwritten laws stating that, if a borrower doesn't demand the return of an item, the ownership will lapse. In this way he acquired all sorts of farming implements, without remembering to whom they belonged, and the neighbours were too scared to attempt to have them returned. Reb Kalmen was a learned man, versed in Jewish teachings, but in matters secular he lacked refinement. Now, some might say that his behaviour hinged on criminality, but in Tchorna Tisa we made allowances. So he manipulated the rules a little to suit his purpose — well, didn't everybody? Now, in spite of all these quirks, Reb Kalmen had a good sense of humour, and endearing qualities.

If my memory serves me right, there were five children in the Jahr family — three daughters and two sons, all of my mother's vintage. The two eldest daughters I didn't know; they had migrated to the USA. But Feige, Mendl and Zayde lived next door to us when I was young. At that time I was an avid stamp collector, and dear Feige was the lucky recipient of correspondence from the USA. She would keep all the old letters and envelopes in shoe-boxes, and I was anxious to get my hands on the stamps. But the competition was fierce. All the Jewish kids in the neighbourhood were avid stamp collectors, and Feige would make us perform menial tasks before parting with any of the stamps. I recall cleaning the stable, wheeling the manure into the field, chopping the wood and tidying the courtyard, all for a few precious American stamps. Then I traded these stamps in Jasina, for other priceless items.

Feige had a ladies bike, and certainly knew how to extract the best bargains for a ride on it. It was the only bike in the neighbourhood, and the bargains were not cheap. She used to think up jobs that hadn't even been invented yet. Within a few minutes, there would be a crowd of kids queuing for bike rides. Gradually, those jobs would become more complex, involving work in the fields at harvest time; there were sacks of potatoes to be carted to the cellar, enormous piles of hay to be fed into the loft, and a lot of household duties to be performed before the bicycle would make its appearance. By the time I got my turn on that bike, I was too exhausted to ride it.

Then there was another problem, and it concerned my long trousers, which had been especially fabricated by my dear grandmother. One leg always seemed to get caught in the bicycle gears, and the trousers would be mangled. I was anxious to get the bike, but the torn trousers presented problems. My mother even warned me not go on that bike, but how could I keep away from it? All the kids queued for it and I couldn't be the exception. So I rode the bike and put on the torn pants for school the next morning, and into the bargain got a terrible hiding from my mother. So I learned whenever mother was around I didn't venture onto the bike; but when she was gone, I was back on it: my dear grandma was so much softer.

Feige, my mother's contemporary, often enjoyed mens company, and she wasn't averse to a little hanky-panky in the fields either. Well, this was a situation I often envied, but was never able to benefit from. So the next best thing was to climb a leafy tree and educate myself in the artful ways of lovemaking. My position in the tree and the excitement both made the situation precarious, but the activities on the ground provided all the entertainment necessary.

Reb Benzin's son Hersh, three years my senior, enlightened me about all the important sexual matters. He was my repository of knowledge, and his explanations were quite invaluable. It was, you might say, a higher education in matters of the heart, and Feige unknowingly provided all the practical tutorials. Well, I am grateful to both of them for ensuring that my sexual education did not get left behind. Without their tuition, I would still have been groping in the dark.

Neither of the Jahr parents endured the Nazi Holocaust; they had both died some years earlier. Feige lost her two brothers, Mendl and Zeide, in Auschwitz. She survived the Holocaust and never returned to Tchorna Tisa. Then some years later I did meet dear Feige in Prague, where she worked as a hospital orderly. She ultimately joined her sisters in the USA.

In 1982, when I went to present a radiography paper at a conference in Jamaica, I decided to visit Cila (Silke) Wald, Reb Kalmen's sister, in Brooklyn, USA. There I got the surprise of my life. Among the invited guests was Feige Jahr. Now, Cila hadn't warned me that Feige Jahr was going to be there, and I was stunned when she arrived. When I saw her the tears began flowing and would not stop. Forty-three years earlier, we had been next-door neighbours. Oh dear G-d, Feige had spent as much time in our house as she had in hers. So this was a re-union to end all reunions, and the tears of joy just flowed … Feige and I were in each other's arms, and didn't leave each other's side for most of the evening. Oh, we reminisced and cried all evening as we recalled people we had once known. Apart from Feige, there were also class-mates of mine at Cila's whom I hadn't seen in more than 40 years.

So the visit to Cila's place was unforgettable; having Feige there was a stroke of genius on Cila's part. I am so grateful to cousin Cila for that unforgettable opportunity. When I think of all the times Feige saved my hide: she used to accompany me home whenever mother was en-raged. Ah, she was a priceless friend, and this was the sweetest reunion imaginable.

The Holocaust 40 years earlier had not altered Feige's lively personal-ity. She was as bright and cheerful as I remembered her in Tchorna Tisa. I so cherished the few hours we spent in each other's company.

When I next visited my mother in Israel, I told her all about the won-derful reunion in Brooklyn, and enjoyed that event all over again. Sometime later, my mother relayed the bad news to me that our dear Feige Jahr had passed away.

Well, I owe Feige a big debt of gratitude for saving my hide so many times. Now all I can say is that I hope her wonderful soul enjoys eter-nal peace in Heaven … Amen.

Chapter 17

Houses of worship

We in Tchorna Tisa never experienced the problems of Jews deserting their religion or the congregation. All we ever aimed for was a *minyon*, so that the *Shabbes* services could proceed without a hitch. There were times when pre-Barmitzvah boys had to be used for a *minyon*. I found that these religious necessities actually moulded our small congregation, and Jews thought deep and hard before absenting themselves from a *Shabbes* service. Friendship and generosity of spirit all played a part, and even chronic illnesses were postponed when an important celebration was looming.

We had our own Saturday morning Shule service, gathering for the *Shabbes* prayers at the Halm-Katz abode. This communal edifice belonged to my great-grandmother Bruche's brother, Yosel Halm. There we had a single, communal Torah, used for all festive occasions; in addition to *Shabbes* we also observed all other Holy Days there. Reb Yosel and his family lived near the Behensky Bridge. This bridge was located half-way between Tchorna Tisa and Jasina.

Mind you, had we had the requisite ten men in Tchorna Tisa every Saturday, then I would have been trotting to *Shule* for *Shacharit, Mincha* and *Maariv*[17]. But as it was, we never knew if a *minyon* was going to be present.

---

17   Shacharit - morning service, Mincha - evening service and Maariv - afternoon service. In many communities Mincha and Maariv are recited back-to-back so a second visit to the synagogue or Temple is not required on the same day. Wikepedia

Anyway, on *Shabbes* and most other Jewish Holy days, Reb Yosel's house was abuzz with excitement. The lounge room was converted into a house of prayer, and the Torah (with its collection of commandments) materialised from behind the curtain, to assume pride of place. But if there was no *minyon*, the Torah wasn't opened, and the biblical script wasn't read. So, a few men would often stand outside and rope in any Jew who passed in the street.

A more serious calamity was when a death happened and some people began recounting the bad points of the deceased. We Jews consider it a Mitzvah when the behaviour of the deceased is favourable. There, we dispensed with judgement on the deceased long before he even hit the grave. So the Almighty was always the first to pass judgement on the soul. I would say, under the circumstances, the most appropriate thing would have been for the Tchorna Tisa Jews never to die.

Now, Reb Yosel, whom I remember as an entertaining gentleman, had a mischievous smile and a long white beard. In his youth, he flirted with and subsequently married Silke, the sister of our next-door neighbour Kalmen. But Kalmen had never broadcast the fact that he had a sister named Silke, or that he was born in Mikolicz, Poland. Reb Yosel and Silke lived together in their house near the Behensky Bridge for a good few years.

Together they had four children, named Sure-Yente, Mendl, Bince and Feige. At the age of 60, poor Silke passed away, and it was said that Reb Yosel lived for another 36 years, passing away in 1936.

After Yosel's death, his daughter Bince and her husband Levi Katz inherited the house and property, and the prayers continued there. I must say that our tiny community was fairly cohesive, and it had to be, or we would not have had a *minyon* for our festivals. Of course, if one of the faithfuls had to go to another synagogue, prior arrangements had to be made to secure a Jewish quorum at our own synagogue, so that the service could continue unabated.

Reb Yosel didn't take part in World War I, though there was compulsory military service during the time of the Austro-Hungarian Monarchy. The Chassidic Jews considered a three-year stint in the Monarchy's army a pretty onerous patriotic duty, and even the non-Chassidic Jews regarded the time in the Austro-Hungarian services as a 'non-urgent' priority. Reb Yosel amputated his right index finger, with an axe, it was said — it was the talk of the town. There were rumours that this had been done to make him ineligible for the Kaiser's National Service.

My great-grandmother's brother Moishe, unlike his brother Yosel, never dabbled in matters military. He was more of an ideas man, who busied himself with constructing brick stoves and fabricating ovens for the Tchorna Tisa households. Reb Moishe, from all accounts, was married more than once; he had a son named Chaim-Wolf, but I don't know what happened to him. Anyway, Reb Moishe then married a girl named Golde, and this marriage was more prosperous; together they had seven children: five daughters and two sons.

A most tragic story comes to mind. Golde, anticipating yet another pogrom, secreted her seven young children, but not herself. She was pursued by Russian Cossacks, and in sheer desperation, dived into an icy lake and remained hidden there until the Cossacks left the area. Then, frozen and wet, she attempted to get to her children, but never made it; her strength was giving out, and she knocked on the door to ask for help. Recuperating in the house, Golde developed pneumonia, and died. Now the seven little orphans had to fend for themselves as best they could. They managed despite great difficulty, and some even made it to the USA. However, the ones left behind eventually perished in the Holocaust.

Moishe's son Yechil took an urgent trip to the USA just as World War I raged in Europe; this only goes to show that the Jews were uninspired by Franz Josef's reign and his devotion to duty. After all, the Empire had existed for a thousand years before. But many felt that it had served its purpose — enough was enough. Actually, Franz Josef's monarchy was quite moderate, but it failed to withstand the effects of World War I. I would say that everything that happened was due to my ancestors letting the old Emperor down. Had they gathered and fought the enemy, the Austro-Hungarian Empire would still be hale and hearty today.

In Jasina, three kilometres away from Reb Yosel's place, the religious life was much more intense. Though there was a united community, there were two large dedicated *Shules*; They both conducted daily services, and followed the same religion, but during religious festivals, the membership of one simply ignored the other. The two synagogues, the new and the old, almost faced each other, but that was as far as the reciprocity went. They were both orthodox, but in all other respects one was a bit more orthodox than the other.

Chapter 18

A mostly peaceful co-existence

Y ou may well wonder what life was like in Tchorna Tisa in the early 1940s. Well, we had a mixture of balabatim (the wealthy Jews), the in-between Jews, and the outright poor (we were among them). The rich included professional Jews and business owners who lived on the fat of the land while the rest of the community eked out a tiresome living. Business in Jasina was mostly in Jewish hands, and ranged from large saw mills to clothing factories, household utensils, mixed paper products and small fruit stalls. Nobody seemed extremely rich other than perhaps the two general practitioners, Bach and Tendler. The Jews of Tchorna Tisa were few in number, and did not own any large tracts of land. Essentially, they lived a Jewish life, and most of them observed the Holy *Shabbes*.

Tchorna Tisa was far removed from the seat of Government and law-making. It was the eastern most extremity of the Czechoslovak Republic, where old habits and prejudices prevailed, and life was ruled by religious fervour, encouraged by a generous helping of superstition. As a Jew, I generally had little to fear in Tchorna Tisa. The Hutsuls were traditional foresters, and their womenfolk tended the farms and raised the children up there in the hills. There was a distinct element of decency among the population when not intoxicated; otherwise they were belligerent. In their drunken stupor, they sang anti-Jewish songs, but it was a good-natured hate; we learned to tolerate it.

We Jews scattered in the hills of Tchorna Tisa were conditioned, and passive in response, to anti-Semitic Jew-baiting. On Sundays, we avoided working our fields, and kept mostly indoors on that day. We never knew how much provocation the priest would have instilled in the flock during the church service. When the services were over there would be drunken brawls in the pub, and we often lowered our window shutters and barricaded the doors to avoid anti-Semitic consequences.

Living as a Jew in Tchorna Tisa was fairly uncomplicated, except when we were accused of killing Christ. The undercurrents were always there, but serious anti-Jewish outbursts were mainly seasonal, usually occurring during the Easter festivities. For us the worst time of the year was always Easter. The Hutsuls were a religious breed, and they enjoyed the various holidays throughout the year, but none more so than Christmas and Easter. The most decorative item on the Easter table was a wooden plate with colourful eggs; our neighbours often gave us some of these eggs, and I guarded them with my life, but we never ate them. They were treasured and admired, but that was as far as it went. Non-Jewish Carpathia still remained at the periphery of our lives.

The Easter festivities were observed with devoted reverence, and the blessing of the men of the cloth was the reward. The churches always used ingenious methods to inflame the passions of their parishioners. It was at Easter that the religious indoctrination was at its most ferocious. Our devout Hutsuls heard from their priests the message, imparted in their holy church: "The wretched Jews killed Christ; they nailed Jesus to the Cross, and for that they must endure eternal damnation". The robed cleric cried from the pulpit, "The Jews killed our Saviour: avenge Jesus Christ!"

Now, this was an inspiring message to the saintly Hutsuls — it was all the parishioners needed to hear. After that, it was bloody retribution. It was also a call to the "pagan" Jews to barricade their houses.

The Hutsuls had no doubt that the Jews had killed Christ, and their descendants had to atone for the horrific crime. To argue that we had not been there 20 centuries earlier only inflamed the situation further. Aged ten, I tried to work out how I had caused the death of Jesus Christ two thousand years before. But there was no rational explanation for this anti-Semitic presumption. It mattered little to them that Jesus was crucified in the Middle East and we in Tchorna Tisa had played no part in the crucifixion. The devoted churchgoers were not receptive to reasoning. Arguments only inflamed their senses. And when the devout were intoxicated, it was a matter of a mixture of religious hatred and invigorating schnapps. When they emerged from the church into the strong sunlight, they all promptly retired to Blimka's pub. In the pub the alcohol took over, so Jews could not win either way.

There is little doubt that the Jews lived in fear whenever the Christians celebrated Easter, because alcohol did strange things to their minds. A few windows were smashed and a number of bearded Jews were assaulted, but then life returned to normal; the drunks sobered up and came back to pay for the damage.

Of course Easter would hardly be Easter without some home-made brew they called *chrenyenka*. If the truth be known, this potent drink was actually watered down by Blimka. As the drinkers became more intoxicated, the less *chrenyenka* there was in their glasses.

There were those who pursued the pub and never made-it-to-the-church-on-time, consuming alcoholic beverages early in the day, on empty stomachs. Then there was a second bunch of drinkers, who preferred to do an honest day's work first, and go to the pub in the evenings. However, both groups blamed the Jews for killing Christ, two thousand years earlier.

Christmas was another matter. It was a time when the mood changed; it was the time of the birth of the Saviour, a benevolent time. Now Jesus materialised as a Jew, and his birthday was celebrated in style. The Hutsuls were suddenly good neighbours, and even shared their abundance with the Jews; even the virulent anti-Semites were now anxious to be hospitable. They gave and received presents, but since this was also the killing season of the pigs, the Jews had to be vigilant. My grandma Bince was often given a sumptuous part of the pig's anatomy, and she accepted it graciously, for to do otherwise would have been an unpardonable insult. Now, if you are wondering what happened to that gift, let me assure you that there were plenty of needy Hutsuls who made good use of it.

I much preferred the Hutsul Christmas to our Chanukah. The tinkling bells of the horses and the Christmas carols had a particular poignancy. On Christmas morning most Hutsuls children went to the religious services, and had their eyes glued to the Heavens. They believed that Saint Nicholas and his eager reindeer travelled the world supplying the obedient children with magic toys. Then, as dawn broke, the children would race to the Christmas tree to find out how generous the Heavenly visitor had been to them.

Even the Jewish children in Tchorna Tisa believed in Father Christmas, and the disappointment was immense when he failed to leave presents in their boots. But Jewish parents usually made up the discrepancy.

I attended a Czech school, and the excitement there at Christmas time was indescribable. It is difficult to explain the overwhelming isolation the Jewish children felt at Christmas time, especially if they attended Christian schools. I was one of these children, and I wanted to experience the excitement of both worlds. I still recall how we decorated our classrooms, and how most of the Jewish kids experienced the same overwhelming excitement as their Christian counterparts. We had very little anti-Semitism in our school, and the Jewish and Christian children co-existed quite happily.

So even I had to have a Christmas tree, and it was decorated in colourful tinsels, but I doubt that Father Christmas ever came near our kitchen, knowing that I was Jewish. My dear grandma did explain to me that Jews did not believe in Father Christmas, but when we had a non-Jewish tenant, he always managed to put something in my stocking.

I did long for presents. It was the anticipation and the sheer excitement that used to get the better of me. I just had to have some presents to take to school so that I wouldn't be left out.

Chapter 19

Superstition for every occasion

The village of Tchorna Tisa was tucked away in the basin of the mountainous peaks and as is the case in most isolated communities, folklore and superstition ruled the day. We were richly endowed on both scores, and I was scared out of my wits.

Although both the Jews and the Hutsuls, were steeped in our respective religions there was always an incantation or two to counteract any untoward manifestations. I remember even my grandma Bince had potions for most eventualities, but they never seemed to help me.

There is a covenant that forbids Jews harming each other. So stepping over another's limb was prohibited. Whenever a plaster cast was noticed, the first question would be: "Who stepped over that limb?" Hardly an indictable offence, but chins wagged all the same. Crossing the street with an empty bucket augured badly for other pedestrians, so one always had to have something in the bucket.

I also remember the distinct prayers we had for a beautiful summer's day, for rainbows, for emptying the bladder, and for success in business or in surviving the winter's flu. I challenge any other religion that caters so generously for all the necessities of life. We fabricated prayers to suit any auspicious occasion, but I am still wondering whether the almighty ever listens to them.

No tears to clothes could be repaired on the wearer's back while the wearer was alive, for fear that the brain might be stitched up in the process. Similarly, shrouds were never repaired, as they ensured immortality. So, to bamboozle the Angel of Death, a thread of cotton was always chewed.

Seeing someone with handlebar eyebrows — eyebrows that run across the upper forehead — would also have unspeakable results. But there was a reliable antidote. Simply put, one had to spit three times over the right shoulder and chant the incantation *Tzooracha*. The meaning of the term *Tzooracha* is not entirely understood, but the incantation worked wonders in Tchorna Tisa.

There was also an exalted trust in the power of the horseshoe. It had to be held in the right hand, spat on three times and swiftly tossed over the right shoulder. Of course, tossing the horseshoe was always a dangerous practice, but if it missed all and sundry, luck was assured. I would use the horseshoe before my school exams, and always kept a horseshoe collection in the backyard.

We maintained that a black cat spelled misfortune when it crossed the path of any citizen who was on their way for a particular purpose. This belief was so entrenched in Tchorna Tisa that people used to return home after such an encounter. I remember having fears of misfortune when encountering a black cat before my school exams, and used to race the cats, to try to have them behind me so they didn't cross my path.

In my time, the Hutsul girls no longer believed that marriages were made in Heaven, and often tried to help nature along. So they had these exotic potions, often helped along by the witches, who were doing a thriving business. The potions had to be gulped down while staring at the full moon, and the intended had to do the same thing. Judging by the number of successful marriages, that potion must have been very potent.

I also recall that the girls used to scatter corn in the chicken yard, and if the handsomest cock nibbled the grains, a marriage would ensue before the year was out. I wonder what happened when a chicken, rather than the cock, gobbled the grains …

Longevity, we believed, was affected by the positioning of furniture in a room. The foot end of the bed could never be positioned in the direction of a door opening, because this would simplify the removal of the corpse.

I owe my life to my ancestors: they had the foresight to acquaint me with all signs of danger and give me the wherewithal to counter them. But I am not going to divulge to all and sundry any of the incantations I inherited. This would mean betraying my ancestors, and I can't do that. It simply wouldn't be proper to disclose the family's secrets: they were given in the strictest confidence. And there is no dedicated witch in the world who would divulge such incantations, no matter how shuddering the consequences might be for not divulging them.

I used incantations for other purposes later in life, like when I took up golf. Well, we have all been there and done that, so don't even pretend that it doesn't happen to you.

Now you may well wonder how I happened to take up golf in my old age. Well, when I retired from the Prince of Wales Hospital in Sydney, Australia, I was given a spanking new set of golf clubs. Then it was a question of either learning to play the game or parting with the clubs. So I decided to acquaint myself with the game. I have been playing golf solidly, for ten years[18], and my game has never improved much. On an overcast day when Moore Park in Sydney is deserted, I can break a hundred— not a bad start for a beginner. But once the crowds arrive, my game falls to pieces. As far as the secret incantations are concerned, they don't help the game at all. In fact, I have learned to my detriment that they actually inhibit the game. Golfing seems just to be about a struggle with your golfing skills, which I never had in the first place.

A game of golf often tempts a temptress, but not me. I know for a fact that the golf-maidens talk to their balls before hitting them, but real golfers never address theirs; and don't use incantations.

---

18   At the time of writing

Chapter 20

More memories

I have many other memories of my childhood in Tchorna Tisa. As a child, I slept with my mother and was in the habit of wetting the bed, even when I passed water just before retiring. Curing this entailed licking the frozen window panes; this was an unfailing antidote, but the cure was often worse than the crime.

Above the bridge in Jasina, on the western side, rain or shine, hail or storm, dear Tzivie was always at her fruit stall. She was a buxom woman, with the same nasal deformity as my grandmother's, but hardly anyone knew how hers had come about. Since these two Jewish women, living six kilometres apart, suffered the same nasal affliction, in my imagination I regarded them as blood sisters. On account of this I hoped that Tzivie might slip me the occasional piece of fruit, but it never happened. Tzivie didn't even know I existed.

Across the street from Tzivie's fruit stall, in addition to the fruit and greenery for sale, we had the *Yarmarok*, or sale of animals, twice a week. As well as horses, cows, sheep and goats, the markets always had something out of the ordinary, and people came from far and wide to sell or trade their goods.

When I was a schoolboy of eight or nine, we used to hatch some pretty hairy mischief, usually consisting of thieving fruit. We honed our skills at school and then descended on the markets, concentrating our ingenuity on the out-of-town fruiterers; we couldn't fool the local breed. But these traders were experienced thief-snatchers and knew all the tricks in the book.

Oh, we plotted and schemed, but for every one of our tricks, the fruiterers had ten of their own. I remember we used to split into groups, and each group would carry a honed stick inside their trousers. The stick had a nail at the end of it, and was produced when the opportunity was ripe, but the traders were always a step ahead of us. Oh, we haggled and argued with the traders over the price, while the chaps with the gadgets performed their tricks. This pilfering trick became an everyday occurrence, but it hardly ever send the fruiterers broke. The methods of our thieving had to be innovative, and change daily. As they say in the classics, "Innovation is the spice of life".

I remember seeking out tiny little springs in the forest and tasting the flowing water from them. The water from one of them smelled of rotten eggs, but was otherwise very refreshing. Well, after consulting a few books, I concluded that the spring had a sulphuric acid taste. Now this was a real discovery, and I told no one about it. My excitement grew, and as I frequented the spring often, I must have swallowed a few microscopic bugs with the water. Soon I noticed that my neck was developing an anterior bulge, and my Czech doctor identified it as inflamed tonsils, and advised me not to drink the water. So I stopped consuming the sulphuric water, which, according to the local witch doctor, cured everything from peptic ulcers to ingrown toe nails; I wished that my grandma Bince was still alive then. She was an alchemist, and often used such things as sulphuric water for her remedial concoctions; she could certainly have advised me, but she had passed away. So I learned to tolerate my swollen tonsils.

In 1948, when I arrived in Sydney, I was examined by a physician, who reported to the Australian Jewish Welfare Society (AJWS) that I needed an urgent tonsillectomy. They booked me into the Royal North Shore Hospital and the resident surgeon there advised the AJWS that I did need the operation, urgently. So it was all arranged, and since I was a charity case, there was no warm bed for me in the ward. I was duly bedded down on the open verandah, and my tonsils were whipped out the next day. Then I was fed ice cream for a few days, and subsequently went on to solids. Mind you, I am still puzzled that I didn't catch pleuritic pneumonia on that open verandah, but that's another story.

Part IV

A precarious life

Chapter 21

A poor boy's lunch

My Czech school finished at lunchtime, and most of the kids were impatient to get to the river ice. But during the cold winter months I had to go to the homes of some rich people in Jasina for lunch. Jasina was a charitable place, and a lot of Jewish households provided hot sit-down lunches for the less fortunate. I was classified as needy lad, and the rich Jewish fraternity would allocate me to various families for the meal.

It was an experience to behold. In some homes, I was treated as a member of the family, while in others I was given a place in the kitchen while the family sat comfortably at the dining-room table. I would eat my food, and disappear. These were embarrassing times, because most of the children were my classmates and pestered me, expecting me to do their homework in return for the feed in their kitchen. The whole school knew that I was a charity case. Well, I hope these childhood trials and tribulations have made me a more compassionate human being.

On schooldays, after lunch with a rich family in Jasina , I would go on to Cheder classes from 3pm to 6pm. My school afternoons were taken up with these classes, where I learnt to read and write in Hebrew and learn the Hebrew prayers, but this wasn't as simple as it sounds. We had to translate the ancient Hebrew sentences into comprehensible Yiddish.

Cheder was supposed to prepare me for life — Jewishness with dignity and decorum — but because we were poor, my Cheder classes were financed by the community. I was known as a public pupil, and was whacked frequently, while the privately financed students were molly-coddled. Well, as a result of this, my Cheder suffered and my Hebrew reading hardly ever improved.

My billeting to different households for lunch was a hindrance, because I used to arrive at Cheder late from them, hence giving the *melamed* more opportunities to chastise me. Well, I could do nothing about that; I couldn't very well tell the people when they should feed me. However, the *melamed* saw red whenever I was late, and seldom waited for any explanations. His walking stick was already up in the air as soon as I walked into the Cheder. Consequently, no matter what occurred in that blessed Cheder, I always received punishment.

My Boobe Bince was most embarrassed that I had to accept charity lunches in private homes. She believed that there were always more deserving children, but did they live six kilometres away from school? Though she was too proud to accept handouts, there were times when we really were in need.

I remember once going on a school outing to Tchorna Tisa, and seeing my dear grandma waiting in the street to watch me pass. She waved but I was too embarrassed to acknowledge her. Instead of rushing to embrace my darling grandma, I walked past her in silence. It was an unforgivable act on my part, and spoiled a lovely spring day for me. Then, to top it all, one of my classmates wanted to know if that lady was my grandmother. I nodded bashfully, and he reprimanded me. The memory of this incident has haunted me ever since. Time and time again I ask myself why I did this hurtful thing to my granny, whom I loved so much? Was it because I was embarrassed of her, or was it to cause immeasurable pain to my dear granny? We often do these stupid things without even thinking.

Unlike the other households where I was offered lunch, in my cousin Yoshka's household I was always treated as a member of the family. I often ate hot lunches with them at the table. Yoshka's young wife was an excellent cook, and very generous with the red paprika powder and the meat dishes. Yoshka was the son of my uncle Yance; Yance was one of the five children of my mother's father from his first marriage: Yance, Yidde, Hersh, Adele and Dori. When his wife died, he married my Boobe Bince, while Yance, Yidde, Hersh, Adele and Dori lived with their grandparents in Lazeshtina. All these children maintained a relationship, albeit from a distance, with Boobe Bince, and rightly so. I remember there was an old shoe box where we stacked all the old family photographs, and among them were pictures of Yidde and Hersh, who by now resided in Timisoara, Romania, while the two sisters, Adele and Dori, had migrated to the USA.

Yance married a widow named Hermina, and Yoshka, who lived near the iron bridge, was her son from a previous marriage. He had a prosperous tailoring business, and though he had a markedly shorter right leg, this never affected his tailoring output. The sewing machines were always rattling as if there was no incapacitation at all.

At the time, Hermina and Yance, were living on the same side of the bridge, next to Kaminer's barber shop. Their ground floor residence was small and dark, but chock-a-block with fabulous display crystals and china figurines. I was terrified of touching any of the porcelain crystals for fear of dropping them — they were so delicate and irreplaceable. In those days, I was a restless youngster, and seldom allowed into the inner sanctum to see the valuable porcelain collections.

Uncle Yance's marriage to Hermina was rather submerged in mystery. She was so delicate and refined, and he was a rugged individual, a typical forester. He used to work a six-day week, and seldom observed any of the Jewish festivals. Because of this, I wasn't even allowed to acknowledge him on Saturday afternoons; I had clear instructions from my grandma to look the other way whenever uncle Yance and his horses descended from the forest. However, I remember secreting myself up in the loft, and seeing uncle Yance and his horses pass our house.

While perusing a box of old photographs at home, I came across one of a handsome man my mother told me was Yance's brother, uncle Yidde Tessler. I treasured the photograph, especially because it showed Uncle Yidde astride a shiny new motorbike, which I aspired to own someday. Uncle Yidde was young and handsome in the photograph, just the strident uncle I hoped to have, but he lived in Romania and we resided in Tchorna Tisa. There, though we had plenty of horse-drawn vehicles and oxen on the road, we never saw any motor bikes, and cars seldom graced the dusty streets.

Uncle Yidde's shiny motorbike occupied an honoured place in our old household. It hardly mattered to me that the photograph was 20 years old and that uncle Yidde was probably driving a magnificent motor car by this time. He was an important timber merchant, with a fleet of frisky horses and shiny motor cars. Even his brother Hersh was employed by him; of the three siblings, uncle Hersh was the most timid one.

The same box of goodies also contained photographs of the aunties, Adele and Dori, fashionably fitted out in their 1920s adornments — American style.

Although the five children were blood brothers and sisters, no one could actually swear on a stack of bibles that they were. In those days, the parents of Jewish marriages retained their single names, and the children were split up between them. This was common in those days, when the marriages were performed by the local Rabbi and the husband and wife still retained their former surnames Even if the marriage was a bad one, the offspring still retained the last name of the parent originally allocated. An exceedingly democratic practice, but hardly binding in the dogmatic Christian world. Anyway, this was how the Eisikovits/Tessler offspring were destined to carry their surnames into posterity. It was a biblical phenomenon, still quite common even during my childhood in Tchorna Tisa. I gather there was no compulsion to acquire a husband's surname after the marriage. Well, in Chassidic households, this was an established biblical practice, and no one dared to question it.

At the beginning of the war, Uncle Yance, Aunt Hermina, Yoshka and his dear family were all taken away to Poland and murdered. From memory, we maintained no contact with the Tessler brood in Romania after Avrom-Wolf's demise in March 1929.

Nowadays, the ancient tenet of giving a child the mother's last name is again being vigorously pursued by the feminists. But were they the ones to discover this practice? That is the question. It is rather fascinating that all of these adherents to divergent beliefs find commonality in the practices of ancient Judaism!

But this practice of equality only applies to the Jewish surnames, and in all other respects the Jewish husband still rules-the-roost and is the master of his house, while the wife is the subservient slave. It is he who has exclusive access to the Almighty, and can expect reverence from his brood at home. Even masturbation is a prohibited practice in the Chasidic life, so the children are married off early, and the wives are kept in a perpetual state of pregnancy.

Chapter 22

Always in trouble

During my unhappy childhood, my relationship with my Boobe Bince fluctuated; I soon became aware of her skinny arms and the punishments they could inflict. I remember folding my arms to protect my head when grandma's temperamental elbows handed out punishments. Now I never committed any of my misdemeanours deliberately, but my Boobe Bince didn't see it in that light. She felt I was trying to injure her delicate forearms, and they did get bruised during the altercations. At that point she decided not to punish me, and save up all my misdemeanours until the end of the year, when my mother returned.

When mother came home she never mucked around; she invariably found a sizeable tree-branch and laid into me, until it disintegrated in her hands. She had an awfully vicious temper, and I never looked forward to her return. Whenever she was at home, I always wished to be somewhere else. Sometimes I used to plead with Boobe Bince not to tell my mother about my misdemeanours, but her daughter had a knack of extracting the information anyway. So she would work herself up into an uncontrolled rage, and corporal punishment would follow. Oh, those annual intervals of my mother's homecoming were the death of me; I never looked forward to them.

While my mother was away, she would bring me presents every time she came home. I remember that when I was a lad in first class, after a lot of nagging she bought me a pair of rubber boots. The boots were too small, two sizes too small, but I was so thrilled to have them that I never told anyone about this. Divulging this fact would have deprived me of them. I had never had rubber boots before, and these were my proudest possession in spite of their size. I feared that Bata would not have a larger size, and I was simply too frightened that I might never get another pair, so I wore them while walking much of the time in wet ditches to get some relief and soothe my aching feet. Had I told my mother, she would have taken them back. I remember walking to school in those boots even on the hottest days; I was in love with my boots.

The nails of my big toes became infected and literally fell off, but still I hung on to the blessed boots. Then finally my mother realised that the boots were too small. Now I nurse a mighty bunion on the right foot, and my right big toe rests at a 45 degree angle — and all because of that rubber boot in my childhood.

Another perennial problem I had concerned my friends, who derived particular pleasure from either frightening me to death or beating me to a pulp. I remember they used to lie in wait, and I never knew whether it was going to be a friendly or scary encounter. Once they even came armed with a sharpened stick, and it got lodged in my head. The blood was oozing everywhere, but the culprits vanished.

I wasn't a clumsy lad, but having to carry all of these encumbrances did limit the use of my arms, and consequently I never learned how to defend myself. However, I did excel at school; my grades were always good. I am sure it all had to do with the attention I received from the teachers throughout my primary years.

Chapter 23

My bar mitzvah

In 1938, when I was barely twelve, I finished primary school and enrolled in the high school, which was closer to my home, located just where the pedestrians and the vehicular traffic split in Tchorna Tisa. We had a short cut that often became a raging river in the rainy season.

My Bar Mitzvah was rapidly approaching, and my mother was beside herself with worry. The Bar Mitzvah, I was told, was even more important than the nuptials. On a personal basis I was prepared to be a man, but my Torah readings left much to be desired. Oh, the shame was simply unbearable, and not even the cakes and beverages to celebrate were likely to make up for it.

In times of crisis my family put all their trust in Azriel Feldman from Ternava, married to my grandmother's cousin Blimka. Unlike his contemporaries, Azriel featured no beard or payes — still, if G-dly matters were involved, he was the one to turn to for help. If the Bar Mitzvah boy didn't know his *parsha*, or Torah portion, Azriel would be there to lend a helping hand. So my mother went to Azriel. Both Blimka and Azriel were wonderful people. We often relied on their generosity, and they never let us down.

Azriel believed that a glass of schnapps and a friendly chat would solve everything; he was probably right. However, there was one issue in 1938 that even an alcoholic beverage couldn't fix, and that was my Bar Mitzvah.

Azriel had a *krchma*, a pub — which, if the truth be known, was Blimka's inheritance —separated from us by Pinchuk's land and Benzin's land. Tchorna Tisa was a small country town, and trading hours were displayed, but hardly ever obeyed. The *krchma* traded, legally or otherwise, whenever there were customers, and in the process accumulated vast numbers of debtors who, in their inebriated state, were not eager to pay. Sometimes, Azriel simply turned off the taps, and told everyone to leave.

In their sober state the Hutsuls were model citizens and always paid their debts, but when they were inebriated their good nature turned nasty. A few tumblers of *horiuka* were enough to change a man's personality — but Azriel's unfailing ability to remember the debts helped. Though dozens of inebriated individuals owed him money at any one time, he always remembered their alcohol consumption, and the pub never went broke.

Azriel was often the Angel of Mercy when calamity befell a Jewish household in Tchorna Tisa. Since Tchorna Tisa did not have any street lighting or telephone facilities in those days, complications were often many and varied. Our town was devoid of doctors, nursing sisters and pharmacists — though we did have plenty of good-natured soothsayers and witch doctors. But, for the real life-saving facilities, we had to ingratiate ourselves with Azriel Feldman. He was a remarkable human being. He would often pedal six kilometres in one direction to fetch a doctor or get a prescription filled.

One of Azriel's failings, however, was that he didn't carry any handkerchiefs, and his shirt sleeve used to get very grubby indeed. Another was his rather flirtatious nature; he used to guard the hay near the Douzhena bridge, and often got himself entangled with Marika from next door.

Quite apart from helping to meet the medical needs of his neighbourhood, Azriel was there when calving occurred, when the fences needed mending, or when the rain threatened the harvest. He was also there when neighbourly disputes broke out, or family arguments blighted the landscape.

He was there when it was only three weeks to my Bar Mitzvah, and I still needed to learn my parsha. Learning such a long segment in just three weeks was more than I could do. But the more I studied, the less I knew. I persevered with Azriel's help.

Then in no time the appointed Saturday arrived. The Katzes' abode was converted into a site for the celebration of my Bar Mitzvah.

Everybody seemed nervous. But then, performing before a pious gathering is always a difficult undertaking. My mind was a blank; the lines kept merging before my very eyes. Barely enunciating the words, I managed to get through the reading, hoping against hope that my little family wouldn't be overly ashamed. I recall Azriel was very relieved.

Anyway, I was glad when it was over, and a lavish *kiddush* followed the service. Was anyone proud of me, I wonder? Or did it just seem like yet another *simcha*?[1] I will never know. Now, at last, I was a fully-fledged Jew, in the religious sense, and even went up a notch or two in the eyes of the little local girls. Little did they realise that my lower gear wasn't up to scratch yet. I realised that in biblical times, thirteen-year-olds were already betrothed, or at least spoken for.

Many years later, I was elected President of the Kingsford–Maroubra Synagogue in Sydney, though I had neither the religious background nor the illustrious upbringing required for the Presidency. My only claim to fame was that I had been on the Board of Management for a good few years.

My mind went back to the day of my Bar Mitzvah in Tchorna Tisa. I compared my humble congregation in Tchorna Tisa with that of Maroubra — and there was no comparison. Maroubra, at its full capacity, was probably 20 times larger than Tchorna Tisa, but during the weekday services we would scrounge around for a minyan as we had in Tchorna Tisa.

---

1   Celebration

I kept recalling my own modest simcha in Tchorna Tisa, where grandma prepared the *kiddush* and I was so proud of her. Our invitations in Tchorna Tisa were simply extended by my Grandma's word of mouth.

The Maroubra functions were professionally catered. Sometimes there was even a four-piece band, and the whole affair assumed coronation proportions. The communal hall was often inadequate for the banquets. Some people even took out sizeable bank loans, to satisfy a humble Bar Mitzvah or impress a few business competitors.

Chapter 24

In the darkness

We inherited our land from Boobe Bruche, which was the same land she took possession of from her parents. In the old days, she said, all was impenetrable undergrowth, and the wildlife roamed around, uninhibited; people seldom ventured out at night.

But even in my day, with most of the land already subdivided and fenced off, and with all the wooden bridges and mod cons, Tchorna Tisa was still sparsely populated. People preferred to leave plenty of space between their houses. Another seeming obsession was to build on the crest of a hill, and there were plenty of them around.

In the depth of winter, life was pretty lonely up there, and the wild animals did not make it any easier. At night the hungry wolves and bears would descend from their high grounds in the pine forests, and roam around the neighbourhood in search of food. The most persistent ones even came and sniffed around the stables, which put the fear of God into our animals. The hungry wild foxes also scared the chickens in their coops, and emptied the coops even before the owners realised what was happening. The hungry wolves hunted in packs along the frozen Tchorna Tisa river. The wolves, bears and wild pigs fought pitched battles, and by the morning there were bloodstains in the snow. I remember that even the dogs were fearful about venturing out, and used to hide under the beds. The winters instilled terror in this lad who tracked home on his own every night.

I still remember the talk, when I was about nine years old, of a character named Klevetz who was said to roam the forests. He was a dangerous bushranger, who had met his untimely death a few yards away from our house, but seemingly still continued to stalk the neighbourhood. At night, we often saw his ghost along the Tisa River. Another ghostly visitor was Poly Macsek, a deserter from the army who had been a childhood friend of my mother's, and had been slain beside the Tisa River.

We lived near the church cemetery, and I was convinced that this proximity meant restless souls were meandering around the neighbourhood. Most Jews readily acknowledged the supernatural.

I had to set out before daybreak for the six-kilometre walk to school, and return home long after the sun had set. In the winter months the sun would disappear behind the mountains at four in the afternoon and coming home from Cheder after dark, I had to pass the houses of the Christian bereaved in the dead of night. I believed them to be haunted, and having to pass by played havoc with my fertile imagination. Jews rush their dead to the grave expeditiously, but the Christians delayed burials for three days. I had a morbid fear of the dead, and believed all the wild tales I heard. According to some, the troubled souls often remained among the living, finding solace in the empty houses along the street. To my mind, the souls of the deceased were hovering out there for an inordinately long time, often settling old scores before returning to their graves. By all accounts, we also had malicious fairies brooding in the forests, were wolves hibernating in the valleys, and frenzied witches haunting the pastures.

In general, my Jewish background and my superstitious upbringing in Tchorna Tisa taught me to believe in hearty expressions, delicate manners and enduring fallacies. All of them were firmly set, and human beings seldom had the power to alter any of them.

I made my journeys with smelly garlic in my pockets. It was useful to have this to ward off snakes in the summer; further, in Tchorna Tisa an old legend prevailed that garlic could be used as an antidote on all occasions. This was my theory as well, and I stuck to it. I could hardly imagine a wild boar walking away from me because I had garlic on my breath, but I would still rub it into my toast to make my breath vile, believing this would scare away most wild creatures of the human kind. My breath was nothing to trifle with in those days; even my school-friends kept away. And I also kept some bread in my pockets, just in case some of the dogs did not recognise me on my journey early in the morning or late at night.

I was a loner most of the time, but this wasn't due to the garlic: I never got enough sleep, and was too exhausted to play in the yard. The school used to give us large amounts of homework, and apart from this I had to leave home early, carrying cans of milk, cheese and butter to delivered to the customers in Jasina before school. So I never had any time to play, and even if I'd had the time, my breath always had that delicate garlic smell that the other kids disliked.

Chapter 25

Changing times in Czechoslovakia

I want to discuss the birth of Czechoslovakia, which emanated from the Austro-Hungarian monarchy. The Hungarian monarchy flourished for a thousand years, and Podkarpatska Russ —Sub-Carpathian Ruthenia (formerly called Karpatolya) — was under its continuous domination for most of that time. Then in 1918, when World War I ended, the Austro-Hungarian Empire fell apart. The monarchy was defeated, and Austria and Hungary became independent.

The Czechs had been under Austrian rule for the best part of four hundred years, and the Serbs, the Bulgarians and the Romanians had been under Turkish rule. Yet in spite of these upheavals few of the countries lost their national identity, and most yearned to be free. So as soon as the Hungarian monarchy was defeated, the smaller nations grabbed the opportunity to re-establish themselves.

When Masaryk died in 1937, the Jews of Czechoslovakia were 2.6 per cent of the population, but they enjoyed religious freedom far beyond their numbers. Masaryk's Czechoslovakia was respected all over the world, but his untimely death put an abrupt end to it's popularity. His successor, Benes, had very little in common with Masaryk's politics or charisma, and he never enjoyed the old man's prestige.

The Republic of Czechoslovakia was born on 28 October 1918. Karpatolya became part of the new Republic. The country also comprised

Bohemia, Moravia, Silesia and Slovakia. Had there not been a war, the people would still have endured the Austrian monarchy.

Tomas Garigue Masaryk had served in the Austro-Hungarian parliament. He worked tirelessly to regain his country's independence. Then World War I broke out, and Masaryk fled to England. His parliamentary colleagues in Austria sentenced him to death.

However, by war's end, when the monarchy itself crumbled, Masaryk duly returned to his nation and was proclaimed President of the Czechoslovak Republic. Well, we could not have had a more loving and distinguished President. Under his illustrious leadership, Czechoslovakia prospered, and was, to all intends and purposes, an exemplary democracy. In all, the Republic lasted twenty years; the spoken language had a Slavic dialect, which helped enormously in the country's unification.

Now, our town of Jasina was the most Eastern extremity of the Czechoslovak Republic. Seven years after the formation of Czechoslovakia, I arrived on the scene and settled in Jasina ; the district was known as Podkarpatska Russ. At that time, I was barely six months old.

At home we spoke Yiddish and Ruthenian, but my schooling enabled me to converse in Czech, and my loyalties to the Republic were beyond reproach. Tomas Garrigue Masaryk was my beloved President, and he could do no wrong.

Masaryk became the father of the nation and the conscience of the world. He commanded enormous respect in all international forums, and especially within the League of Nations. He remained at the helm for seventeen years. The Czech people loved his kind disposition, his philosophies and his teachings. Then his health failed and he retired in 1935, but his political influence lived on.

Two years later, on 14 September 1937, when I was twelve years of age, an insurmountable catastrophe happened — our beloved Masaryk passed away! The loss of the illustrious founder of the Republic affected me like nothing else ever had. The nation grieved, mourning its father. I remember his school portrait was lowered, and draped in black. Candles flickered in his memory. I still recall the President's kindly bearded face adorning our classroom; oh, how I cried for him.

His portrait enjoyed a place of honour in every Czech household. At school we read his poetry, memorised his wisdom, and knew that there was no one else like him. A great many other nations also mourned his untimely death, and came to pay homage at his funeral. The man has gone, but his precious legacy lives on forever.

It may seem strange, but even in the darkest hours of my life, I drew strength and inspiration from Masaryk's face. I remembered him in Auschwitz, where the Nazis decimated my people. Tomas Masaryk gave me courage and strength; he still remains my trusted friend ... will there ever be another like him?

Then Dr Eduard Benes assumed the Presidency, and our political fortunes changed for the worse. Benes was a National Socialist, and had totally different aspirations.

My mother, being educated in the Austro-Hungarian mould, felt she owed no particular loyalty to either of the presidents. Her three years of school barely taught her to read, but her cultivated Hungarian often got her out of difficulties. Though her writing never really improved, her loyalty to the Crown was beyond reproach. My mother firmly believed that Hungary could do no wrong. If anyone ever dared to utter a bad word against her Kingdom, a tirade of abuse would follow. She spoke some Czech, but often mixed in Ruthenian words which had nothing to do with the subject under discussion.

Then in 1938, the Czechoslovak Republic was divided up into three different parts: the Czech Lands were taken by the Nazis; Slovakia became a German dependency, and the Ukrainian Sitchak brigade ruled Podkarpatska Russ, then known as Zakarpatska Ukraina — the land mass between the regional capital of Uzhorod and Jasina ; their loyalties were with Nazi Germany. This Ukrainian aberration had come into being as soon as Hitler dismembered Czechoslovakia; it remained in existence for six months before the Hungarian army put an end to it.

When the Nazis demanded the Sudetenland, Benes obliged, abdicating from his position as president of Czechoslovakia on 5 October 1938. After the abdication of Benes, General Jan Syrovy formed a caretaker government. As the Kristallnacht pogroms against the Jews started in Germany, the Czechs were busy installing Emil Hacha as their President of a divided Czecho-Slovakia.

Meanwhile, in March 1939, Slovakia seceded from the Republic and Germany occupied Czech Bohemia and Moravia. The faithful Ukrainians in Sub-Carpathian Ruthenia also tried to establish their little heaven on Earth, but Nazi Germany promised the territory to Hungary; the Ukrainians went ahead just the same. Then three days later Baron von Neurath, the Reich's Protector of Bohemia and Moravia, settled the matter; he occupied the Czech territories while Emil Hacha was President. At the same time, across the border, Adolf Hitler was installed as Chancellor of Germany, and there were celebrations all round. The German occupation of the Czech Lands also negated the iron-clad treaties with France and England; Prime Minister Chamberlain even went to Berlin to arrange the surrender of Czechoslovakia. So in short, the Czech Republic was sacrificed to expediency — a single sheet of paper declared the 'Peace in our Time'. Chamberlain claimed that this 'blatant treachery' was committed to prevent World War II, but it hardly achieved that. World War II was actually accelerated by it. So Nazi Germany enslaved the Czech territories and bit by bit, the whole of Europe; the extermination of the Jews was then a foregone conclusion.

The German Chancellor marched into Czechoslovakia and although the Czechs were armed to the teeth, not a single shot was fired in anger from the Czechoslovakian side. The occupation of the Czech Lands was smooth, and you may well ask: "Where were the allies?" Oh, they were still debating the Treaty that assured Czechoslovakia of their help.

Slovakia was apportioned to Jozef Tiso, who formed a Government in Bratislava in March 1939, and Podkarpatska Russ was given to the Ukrainians and became known as Zakarpatska Ukraina. Under Tiso, Slovakia proclaimed its independence and promptly became a Nazi stooge. The demise and the sequestration of the Czechoslovak Republic therefore happened quite swiftly.

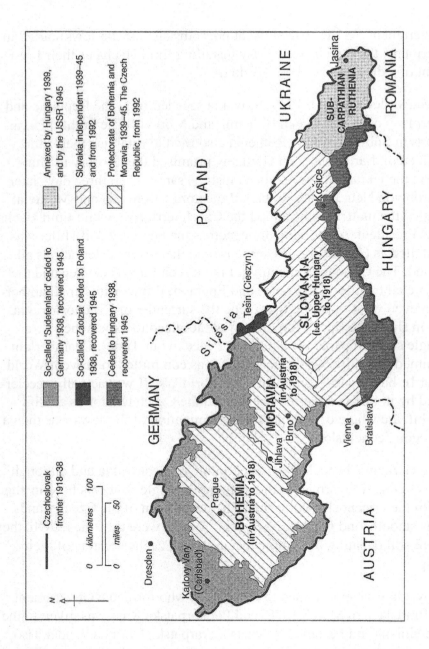

Czechoslovak
frontier 1918–38

So-called 'Sudetenland' ceded to
Germany 1938, recovered 1945

So-called 'Zaolzia' ceded to Poland
1938, recovered 1945

Ceded to Hungary 1938,
recovered 1945

Annexed by Hungary 1939,
and by the USSR 1945

Slovakia independent 1939–45
and from 1992

Protectorate of Bohemia and
Moravia, 1939–45. The Czech
Republic, from 1992

GERMANY

POLAND

UKRAINE

ROMANIA

HUNGARY

AUSTRIA

SUB-
CARPATHIAN
RUTHENIA

SLOVAKIA
(i.e. Upper Hungary
to 1918)

MORAVIA
(in Austria
to 1918)

BOHEMIA
(in Austria to 1918)

S i l e s i a

Tešín (Cieszyn)

Jasina

Košice

Brno

Jihlava

Prague

Karlovy Vary
(Carlsbad)

Dresden

Vienna

Bratislava

kilometres   100

miles   50

0   50

0

N

The *Zakarpatska Ukraina Sich* forces[2] threw their lot in with the
Nazis. The Ukrainians ardently supported Hitler, and enthusiastically
endorsed the Jewish Holocaust. In return, the Nazi regime viewed

2   The Carpathian Sich were irregular soldiers of the short-lived state of Carpatho-
Ukraine

136

with favour the establishment of an Independent Ukrainian State in Carpathia, after the disintegration of Czechoslovakia; However, this enthusiastic activity did not sit too well with the Hungarians, who still considered Karpatolya their territory. After all, Karpatolya had been part of the Austro-Hungarian Empire for a thousand years. As it happened, Nazi Germany also viewed the Hungarian forces activities with a jaundiced eye, but they needed them on the Russian Front.

Chapter 26

Life in Zakarpatska Ukraina

D uring my first year of high school I excelled in my studies and
was quite a popular student. I had blossomed in my Czech
public schooling, and was grateful to my mother for sending
me there. In November 1938 only two months into my second year of
high school, the Ukrainians took over and promptly expelled the Jewish students.

Tchorna Tisa was no longer the peaceful district it had once been as
Zakarpatska Ukraina became grossly anti-Semitic. There were young
Ukrainians around who took their orders from the Nazis, and they had
to be avoided at all costs. The young Hutsuls now joined the Ukrainian
Sichaks, and the German Master Race reigned supreme.

The Ukrainian nationalists adopted the slogan of blaming the Jews for
Christ's death, and during the time of World War II they pursued the
Jews through the streets. It became fashionable to kill the Jews, and
the Nazis heartily approved. In other words, this was religious fervour
used for criminal ends. I still remember how the Jews barricaded themselves in their houses while the street violence raged. It was all hy-
pocrisy: the Ukrainians attacked the Jews in the streets, but then they
conveniently retired to the Jewish pub, to gloat about their exploits.
Hardly an appropriate way to celebrate their punishment of the Jews.

The Jews were not entitled to any rations coupons, and the milk deliveries also dried up, so I had to start work. At barely fourteen years old, instead of attending high school I was forced to do a man's job — and earn a pittance for it. I found work in the forestry office, but the position was hardly secure. Every time anyone from the upper management visited, I was dispatched to the stables. Jewish workers were not paid any wages, and so I had to labour under an assumed, Christian name.

My immediate boss was named Tommy Friend. He used to boost my pay packet with overtime pay that I never worked. As his name suggested, he was a wonderful friend, and his love life was equally boundless; he even bedded the boss's wife, without the husband's knowledge. When the Nazis arrived in 1944, and herded all Jews together in the Jewish cemetery, I remember Tommy Friend arriving, in the dead of night, with a generous parcel of food. He pushed it through the barbed wire fence, and duly vanished; that was the last time I saw my dear friend Tommy.

We had a lot of anti-Semitism around us, but the Tisa river harboured no such prejudices and still carried the *darabes* twice a week. One of my jobs was to measure the logs when they came down from the mountains, and stamp the information on them before they were put to rest, at the river's edge.

The stamping of the figures had to be pretty straight. So my team consisted of four people, generally working in harmony. I was the one who marked the logs for the cutters, so that the measurements coincided. Now, squaring the ends of the logs may appear simple, but making the cuts vertical was not for the faint-hearted. One had to have years of experience, and the saw had to be new, but this subtlety was often lost on the inexperienced cutters.

Each log, apart from having its length and average thickness noted, also received a dedicated serial number extracted from my book. I printed these numbers each night, using a noisy little hand-machine, which automatically wetted itself as it returned to its base. This clever machine changed its serial numbers automatically every time it hit the paper, and all I had to do every so often was to replace the saturated pad. I also had to keep in mind never to part with the blessed entry book; mistakes could often be made when you least expected. Consequently, the book remained in my possession at all times, and the measurements were entered immediately, to avoid any confusion.

I remember the times when my friend Imre and I worked well into the night, swapping our books to check the additions for accuracy; he was a great friend, and a womaniser to boot. He often used to disappear to indulge his fancy in a bit of hanky-panky, and I am convinced that the boss's wife provided all the amusement. The boss Kovacs was always in a drunken stupor, and no woman was ever safe around him. So the social life in the office gave ample scope for in-depth love-making, but I could not participate in any of it. At 16 years of age, I was more interested in the variety of the office guns than in any random pussy-footing.

Most other people went to the pub straight after work, but I first had to convert all my daily measurements into cubic metres. Then I had to add up the measurements on each page, for good measure. My next task was to submit a comprehensive report of all my measurements to the Hungarian office manager. Now, all of this may appear simple and straightforward, but when there were seventy entries to a page and five or six pages per day, it quickly mounted up. I remember walking around like a zombie, with all the figures flashing before my eyes. However, the next morning I had to appear bright and breezy, for there was no time to relax. The spring was almost upon us, and the river had to be cleared of logs before the ice melted — the annual *tourlash* in the river, which came after the winter, waited for no one.

When the snow melted and the mountains and valleys were cleared of the careering logs carried along the river, my job would begin as the only Jewish stable hand who acted as a timber manipulator in Douzhena —or anywhere else, for that matter. There was a lot of abuse, but I began anticipating the job priorities even before I was told what had to be done. This made me a diligent worker, and so I often avoided the snide remarks that could be so hurtful.

In the mountains at the time, we were accommodated in *kolebas*, which was a round wooden structure with a central fireplace, and had an opening through which the smoke could escape. During the night, the howling winds returned the smoke back into the *koleba*, and choked the occupants to death — so to speak. All the forest workers slept in this *koleba*, and quite often there were girls in there as well.

Now, the sleeping arrangements were around the fire, on fresh pine branches, and it was so crowded that we slept on our sides, and when one turned all had to turn. I observed this rule religiously, but some others did not. So, there were 14 virile men, one attractive female, and a Jewish lad. Since I was very much in a minority, you would think they would have given me access to beautiful Paraska, but it never happened. Paraska was the girlfriend of one of the big lads, and I simply had to behave myself. But my friend took full advantage of the fact that he had his girlfriend next to him, and they were at it all night; they had the full-hearted encouragement of all the other occupants.

The spring mornings were still rather freezing and the work I performed was miserable in the wet weather, but the roaring fires were warm. And we were never short of firewood.

Whenever I made the trip down river to Velky Bocskov I wore the mandatory sharp metal shoe attachments for standing safely on the *darabe*. It was an auspicious event, an unforgettable foolishness; who ever heard of a little Jew jumping on a moving *darabe*? It was foolhardy, but I had to prove to myself that I was able to do it. Well, whenever I made the trip, I had the distinct impression that the men developed a new regard for me. They still called me 'the little Jew', but somehow I earned their respect: I made the journey with them.

I even wore the shoe attachments on land. When the moving logs made deep channels in the snow, channels would freeze over at night and become as slippery as hell in the morning.

Now at this stage I was still able to observe my religion and enjoy the luxury of going to the synagogue most Saturdays, but the future looked bleak. Jews with foreign credentials were already being sent to Poland, and the residue thanked the Almighty, every morning, for being spared.

In Tchorna Tisa, the Hutsuls had always obeyed certain unwritten rules, and there was a high degree of tolerance simply because we fulfilled a useful function in a primitive society. However, after the so-called 'more civilised' Ukrainians took over Carpathia, the rule of law fell by the wayside and the notion of independence took hold. This region embraced the Nazi ideology, and now the Jews were in serious trouble. With all the Nazi successes in Eastern Europe, Hitler's forces were expanding their domain, and the Jewish Holocaust was spreading like an irrevocable catastrophe.

In the rest of Europe, all the historic treaties that preceded World War II were proving valueless. There was the USSR Defence Treaty with France that Stalin abrogated, after the demise of Czechoslovakia. He then entered into a ten-year Soviet-German Non-Aggression Pact, but this paralysed the Soviets and accelerated the German occupation of Poland. Then Poland made iron-clad defence treaties with France and Great Britain, but neither lifted a finger when Hitler marched into Poland. Chancellor Hitler appropriately described their rhetoric and indecision as sitzkrieg — roughly, a sitting war. With all this going on, Italy's Mussolini felt left out, and he promptly declared war on France and England. However, Hitler had no time for Mussolini, and soon marched right across Europe, enslaving Norway, Denmark, Holland, Luxembourg and Belgium, and leaving Switzerland, Sweden and Finland as neutral countries. He then conquered Paris on 14 June 1940 and declared France another puppet of the Third Reich. So now the whole of Europe was dancing to the Nazi tune, and Hitler was ecstatic, but in London Chamberlain had doubts, and well he might!

You see, Chamberlain's careful policies and assurances were now in tatters; he was double-crossed by France and most of Europe, so he turned to America. Meanwhile, the German tunes dominated Paris and the patriotic upper classes seemed to welcome Hitler; *Der Zweck heiligt der Mittel* was the slogan of the day — roughly translated, "the end justifies the means."

Chapter 27

Hungarian occupation

The Ukrainians were barely in power for six months when the Hungarian forces occupied Karpatolya on March 16, 1939 and beat the hell out of them — Hungary could not tolerate a Ukrainian entity on its border. The Ukrainians bravely confronted the Hungarians, hoping the Nazis would join them, but the Nazis had more urgent worries on the Russian front. The whole of Europe was now involved in a war.

I still remember how Nazi Germany transported Jews across the Polish border, and told the world how urgent the work was over there. Many of the Jews escaped into the forests and I still remember the Polish and other Jews crossing over into Karpatolya, escaping death in Poland only to be mowed down by the Hungarian soldiers near the border. Hungarian patrols often returned with Jewish blood on their tunics, and the chains they carried were also soaked in Jewish blood; they had used the chains to bind the victims together before they were executed.

However, my mother wouldn't believe any of this. "The Hungarian soldiers would not commit these crimes", she said. She maintained that the Hungarian soldiers must have been attacked, because they would never execute people unnecessarily. How could our own countrymen massacre, maim, gas and burn the Jews? She asked. But these compatriots found outlandish excuses for the massacres, which I never understood; they were beyond comprehension.

And so Karpatolya became a loyal Hungarian province. There were rumours that Nazi Germany was also gathering its troops to occupy Karpatolya. If the truth be known, Nazi Germany had no time for the Hungarians and did prepare to occupy Karpatolya, but the Hungarians were too quick and beat them to it. The Hungarians annexed Karpatolya from the Ukrainians because they believed that it belonged to the Austro-Hungarian Monarchy. Well, the Magyars may have been right. World War I did cause the disintegration of the monarchy, and at that time Carpathia was given to Czechoslovakia; this remained the case for the next 20 years. Then, with Germany's occupation of the Czech Lands, the Republic vanished. So the Magyars incorporated Karpatolya into the Hungarian Motherland and it remained there for some five years, until Nazi Germany invaded in October 1944.

Actually, the Hungarian occupation of Karpatolya surprised the Jews, but the Jews still welcomed the Hungarians with open arms. You see, the Jews expected the Nazis to arrive — and then our days would have been numbered. Most households were preparing themselves to die. Jews were bidding each other farewell, and neighbours in dispute were quickly settling all their differences.

When the Hungarian forces first arrived, the Jews danced in the streets. To the Jews, the fact that the Hungarians beat the Nazi forces by a few hours meant survival. It was simply incredible. One minute we were preparing to die, and the next there was a reprieve. Actually, during those tragic days we lived and died at the same time; the words *Baruch Hashem*, blessed be G-d, never faded from our lips. It didn't matter that the miracle was short-lived — what mattered was that it happened: the Magyars rather than the Germans arrived. As I recall those tragic events of the war, we Jews would have welcomed the devil himself, if he had the power to postpone the inevitable tragedy of the Jewish Holocaust.

When the Hungarian forces occupied our territory, I nurtured some hope that the Hungarians might let me serve in the *Levente*, a young Hungarian militaristic grouping. I practised the customary salute, but little did I know that even this option would be denied to a Jew.

A ruling came that all Jews must report to a depot, to be divided into labour brigades of twenty to thirty and marched through the city streets every morning and evening. Carrying polished shovels their right shoulders, they were forced to sing anti-Semitic Hungarian marching songs. The brigades were pelted with rocks and any other rubbish that could be found. Soon, this became an accepted morning and evening exercise: the Jewish marchers sang, and the obedient inhabitants emptied their stinking chamber pots on them. Oh, life wasn't worth living.

The Hungarian occupation forces wasted no time in imposing curfews on the Jews of Carpathia, but at least we Jews were still alive. Still denied any rations coupons, we had to live on our wits. Then the Hungarians also dispatched the mobilised Jewish labour brigades to the Russian front, where they were slaughtered by the hostile Nazi forces, as well as the friendly Soviet armies; neither side understood the purpose of the Jews being on the Russian front.

For the first three years of the Hungarian occupation I continued my cushy forestry job. Of course, I was still a Jew, and had to hide in the stables every time unexpected visitors came to the office, but for the rest of the time I was out in the forest or converting complex timber measurements into cubic metres.

Everyday Jews were coming across the border to Jasina from Hungary and Poland and being rounded up, then shot. Helping any escaped Jews was punishable by death, but we sometimes hid people in our cellar and the loft in the barn. They would tell us of the terrible atrocities taking place. Many people in Jasina refused to believe them, but I didn't see why they would lie. I felt terrible guilt that I couldn't do anything to stop the carnage.

In 1943 our house was taken over by officers of the Hungarian army, leaving us to sleep in the kitchen, and it became impossible to take in any more escapees.

Chapter 28

Then came the Nazis

Around *Pesach* 1944 the Nazi forces marched into Karpatolya. First the German motorcycles arrived, then the heavy infantry.

I still remember the arrival of the German forces and how the Jews were in two minds about it. Had the Germans come to bolster the Ukrainian resistance against the Hungarian forces, or to finish off the Jews? Either way, we were living on borrowed time. Once the Nazis occupied Karpatolya, they immediately began targeting the Jews and the itinerant Gipsies.

The evidence against the Jews was flimsy. And what was their irrevocable evidence for these crimes? A deliberate fabrication of unsubstantiated lies by that infamous Streicher, whose evidence justified the extermination of the Jews[3]. His lies were made believable by their embellishment. All the cartoons and fallacious blood libels served the Nazi philosophy well; they stoked the flames against the Jews. Streicher claimed that only a Jewish Holocaust would expiate the Jews' crimes against humanity, and Hitler, Streicher and all the other Nazis desired nothing less.

The incessant and systematic propaganda against the Jews began. Jews could no longer travel to foreign lands, and the Gestapo issued

---

3   Julius Streicher was a prominent member of the Nazi Party prior to World War II. He was the founder and publisher of Der Stürmer newspaper, which became a central element of the Nazi propaganda machine. Wikipedia

Durchlassscheine, or exit permits, to those Jews who were prepared to leave their property behind. Then Reich Protector Konstantin von Neurath established the Central Office for Jewish Emigration, the *Zentralstelle*, headed by the commander of the Security Police. In effect, the *Zentralstelle* became the centre for the persecution of the Jews. Reading all the German regulations, I am surprised that any Jews survived the Holocaust at all.

At the time that the Germans wiped Czechoslovakia off the map, I was living in Podkarpatska Russ, and witnessed this disintegration with profound regret. It put an end to my earnest hopes of ever achieving some sort of academic future. Had there been no war, and had Podkarpatska Russ remained Czechoslovakian, I would have achieved great academic heights. But, as it turned out, Hitler's forces were all around us, and my prospects were less than zilch.

It was incomprehensible to me that the Nazis would come to exterminate us while losing the war on all fronts, but this was their precise intention. Had we had a sympathetic population around us, the Jews could have been hidden for a few months, but that was not to be. Although German might was declining by the day and many thousands of the German troops were languishing in Russian prisons, the Fatherland never gave up on the Jews. Even as the Red Army was taking its remnants all the way to Berlin, the Nazis were still taking revenge on the Jews; the gas chambers never stopped functioning.

The Jewish Holocaust overtook the Nazi mentality, and they pursued the Jews to the bitter end. Hitler's Germany had two radical tasks to complete — the first was to win the war. Since Germany was losing World War II, the second task had become urgent: to burn as many Jews as humanly possible.

The Russian winters helped to turn the tide against the Germans and, ultimately, win the war. Actually, from all accounts, there were two wars going on in the Soviet Union: in one, the Germans were fighting for Stalingrad, while in the other the Red Army was running away in Siberia. In the Siberian conflict, the Nazi guns refused to fire owing to the excruciating cold, and it was this that turned the tide. So, while the Soviet propaganda films were showing endless columns of bedraggled Germans retreating, this wasn't far from the truth. I remember seeing a Russian film titled *Six Hours After the War* where the Nazi armies, in utter subjugation, marched backwards. The Soviet Union was victorious, and didn't hesitate to show it!

Once this German retreat started it never ceased; the Nazis simply ran, in their thousands, all the way to Prague and beyond. Even Hitler noticed the beginning of the end, and started contemplating his own demise. There was no 'tomorrow' in the Nazi lexicon! The Fuhrer had set these arduous tasks himself, and the participants were not programmed to cease operations while the task was half completed. In fact, the military losses on the battlefields only exacerbated the urgency in the killing fields: I dare say the Nazi forces anticipated their own defeat and tried very hard to complete the grisly task of extinguishing the Jews. I think they hoped that the world would thank them for a job well done.

My illiterate fellow Jews had only two fervent beliefs: one that the Almighty would adjudicate in Heaven, and the other that the United States of America would rush to the aid of the Jews in Tchorna Tisa. Almost every Jewish family had some relative, close or otherwise, in the distant USA, and believed this was our guarantee of survival. In Tchorna Tisa we heard of Adolf Hitler's incessant ravings, but they hardly caused a ripple. Our immediate fears were about the vocal Ukrainian minority who danced to Hitler's tune. We knew that mighty America would come to our aid, but would this be soon enough? That was the undying question on everyone's lips.

Chapter 29

My grandmother's funeral

My dear grandma, Boobe Bince, expired in her sleep six months before the Germans deported the Jews to Auschwitz. Boobe Bince was born in 1879, and passed away during the Hungarians occupation of Karpatolya, on 5 August 5 1943, at the age of 64 years. We mourned my grandma's passing bitterly, but later realised that she would not have survived the gas-chambers of Auschwitz. She had suffered immeasurably, enduring the pain of seeing her dear lifelong friends being carted away to the killing fields of Poland by the Hungarian occupation forces.

Boobe Bince was a beautiful human being, like her mother, Boobe Bruche. who had passed away in 1935 at the ripe old age of 98. I still recall how Boobe Bruche used to carry on conversations with people she knew but who weren't there. Often I would butt into the conversation, and great-grandma would reply, as if I were part of the discussion. Oh, it was all hilarious. Often she used to drift from one incident to another in her conversation, and her expressions were not always complimentary, but we enjoyed them all the same. She was a grand old lady, who invariably took my part in most arguments, and for this I always loved her.

My dear Boobe Bince was like a thin shadow, but her posture was always upright. She never stooped, even in her advanced years, and she nurtured the piety of strict biblical orthodoxy. Her devotion to matters celestial was ingrained — hers was knowledge straight out of the scriptures. Her generation was illiterate, but that never inhibited my grandmother. She acquired her religious piety from nature, from the things around her.

Her contemporaries also extracted their piety from orthodoxy, by word-of-mouth: this type of knowledge was transmitted down the line in colloquial Yiddish. From one generation to the next, the *Yiddishkeit* and piety went hand-in-hand, in solemn transmission.

Though Boobe Bince was a conventional woman, and uneducated, integrity meant a lot to her, and she was scrupulously honest. To her, G-d's precepts were pure and binding; she always lived by them. This was a pervasive religious attitude that she tried to instil in me, and it certainly rubbed off. My Boobe Bince often borrowed from one neighbour to pay another, just to keep to her beliefs. I remember her account in the grocery store of Hersh and Reesye Bohorodcsaner, and how she borrowed from cousin Blimka. As a result, whenever Boobe Bince needed to borrow something, her reputation preceded her, and she was seldom refused.

Like all Jews in Tchorna Tisa, Boobe Bince was buried in the Tchorna Tisa cemetery. In Tchorna Tisa we had neither the resources nor the inclination to maintain a separate Jewish cemetery, and so the burial ground was the same for all. The Jewish section was halfway up a steep hill, which the bereaved had to clamber up. The approaches to it were either muddy or dusty, depending on the time of year. When it rained, which was often, access to our cemetery was a challenging task, hardly to be undertaken by the faint-hearted.

All the Jewish dead were carried for six kilometres, to the ritual cleansing station at the *Chevra Kadisha* in Jasina , where the prescribed rituals were carried out, then back to the cemetery in Tchorna Tisa. Though the *Chevra Kadisha* did all the necessary things, finding pallbearers was another matter. Our religious Jews would rather walk to the cemetery than accept a lift in a motorised hearse.

Funerals were always solemn affairs in our Orthodox community. Jews were buried before the heat even left their bodies. So we knew nothing of such things as rigor mortis. Anyway, the size of our coffins never varied, and the corpses, often warm, had ample room to get into some indelicate positions, which led to problems when the coffin was being carried.

The Community Elders wisely decided that the front bearers had to be midgets and the back ones giants, to level out the corpse on its way up the hill to the cemetery. However, the learned Rabbi quickly laid down the law, and made the bearers swap positions. This decision caused enormous friction in our orthodox laity. Everyone knew that the bulk of the weight would be in front, but the giants would be at the back. Consequently, orthodoxy being what it is, the learned Jews stubbornly refused to concede, and the situation continued. So we were lucky to get anyone to bear the corpses to the Holy Ground. Then another pertinent question arose: why was the Jewish cemetery up on a hill, where the people had to clamber to get to it? The learned Rabbi maintained that this meant the body was closer to Heaven, and that was as good an answer as any; it may not have been logical, but the Rabbi had spoken! You, see dying in Tchorna Tisa wasn't just a simple matter of expiring ... oh, no!

From the time of the Hungarian occupation, we began to encounter severe problems with the pallbearers: all the able-bodied Jews were now in *munko-szolgalatos* — work detachments — on the Russian Front. When my grandmother died, three old men volunteered to carry her to the cemetery, and I was to be the fourth. In Judaism the mourners are not allowed to carry the dead, but this was wartime, so I carried my granny.

She was buried on a nice, sunny day. I wondered, as we walked, whether she noticed the potholes in the road. I had other questions percolating in my mind at that time, but there was no one to answer them. Most of the learned men who could have answered some of my queries had already been dispatched to Poland. So my questions had to remain unanswered.

The other pall-bearers complained that my grandma's weight was increasing as we carried her. Her cortege crossed two wooden bridges on the way to the cemetery and if the old wives' tale was true, her body absorbed large quantities of water.

We carried her only as far as the Rosenthal abode, because it was here that the three other carriers gave up the ghost. This was still only half-way to the Jewish cemetery, but they simply walked away, and left me in the middle of the road. So here I was, my grandma dead, and not a Jewish male in sight. Never mind that delivering the dead to the grave is one of the greatest good deeds in the Talmud. But our elderly Jews thought of themselves first, and my grandmother's dignity came a poor last.

I approached a Ruthenian, and asked him to kindly let the Jews of Jasina know that there was a Jewish corpse in the middle of the road, outside the Rosenthal place. And soon enough, a contingent of Jews arrived to finish the task. Well, we reached town, in double-quick time, and climbed the hill to the cemetery, where my darling grandma Bince was finally buried.

Then, six months later the rest of us were taken to the Extermination Camp of Auschwitz, leaving my Boobe Bince without a headstone. We were not there to consecrate the headstone one year later as was the Jewish custom.

If there was a single consolation to be had in all of this, then it was the fact that she passed away in her own home; this deserves our eternal thanks. I only wish I could have found her grave in 1992 when Ruth and I revisited the Jewish cemetery.

Part V

Auschwitz to Australia

Chapter 30

On the path to the camps

In April 1944, six months after my grandmother died, the Nazis gathered up all the Jews of Jasina and shipped them off to Auschwitz. There, in the 12 remaining months of the war, they exterminated most of the Jews, and those who survived were unrecognisable skeletons including myself. The Nazis incarceration of the Jews in Auschwitz would not have been so bad had the Nazis not been hellbent on exterminating all the Jews. They had six years to do it in, but I suppose fighting a war against the world and exterminating the Jews at the same time was not such an easy matter.

My first experience of the concentration camps was in Auschwitz in Poland, and then Mauthausen and Ebensee in Austria. In all, I was in the camps for over a year. The camp experiences have remained with me, and no matter what I do in life, the memories of Auschwitz, Mauthausen and Ebensee are there in the recesses of my mind.

My journey to the camps began with the Nazi officers moving into our house during *Pesach*, displacing the Hungarian officers, who had left Mother and myself cramped in the kitchen. I still remember trying to conduct the *Seder* service in whispers, while the drunken Nazi officers played havoc in the next room.

Then, the day after *Pesach*, the SS knocked on the door and told us to take a few belongings and wait in the street. We took food and water and twenty minutes later trucks arrived to collect us. All I can remember of this episode is our little dog, Baby, chasing the Nazi trucks. When the trucks accelerated, our Baby grew tinier, and eventually disappeared in a cloud of dust. A deluge of tears poured down my face as our dog disappeared.

That was the last time I saw my Baby alive.

When the trucks reached Jasina they disgorged us into an enclosure situated below the Jewish cemetery. I recall my deep trepidation on the fateful journey that took us there. Having learned to keep away from the vicious dogs and the rubberised truncheons, I kept huddling in the middle of things, where the crowds were thickest.

We remained there for about a week, hundreds of us, behind barbed wire with only the food and water we had packed, out in the open in the April cold. That first night my Hungarian "friend" threw a bundle of food over the fence—the only act of kindness we received from anyone in Tchorna Tisa. Then the Nazis took us to the railway station and loaded 80 people to each waiting wagon. There were many children as most families had at least four.

We were very conscious whether the train was going to Hungary or, to Poland and certain death. The wagons were sealed and the only way we could get a sense of direction was from the children lying on the floor looking through the space under the door and describing what they saw. There were people in the wagons who had traveled and were familiar with different locations. As it turned out we headed to Hungary at a very slow pace. The train was constantly sidetracked to allow any regular service or express trains to go past. At each stop, one person from each wagon was permitted to go to a tap and get water. People died on the way—the heat and air was oppressive. There was no room for the adults to sit. We leaned on each other and tried to conserve energy. Anger wasn't wasted on trivial things.

After nearly three days travel we found ourselves in a field outside the town of Mateszalka in Hungary. We were marched into an enormous holding camp of around 18,000 Jews.[4] It was reasonably well organized with some food and water provided. The camp in Mateszalka held people from all over eastern Europe, speaking many languages and dialects. I had never heard so many dialects before. In Jasina people spoke only Yiddish, Ruthenian and a smattering of Czech.

And here we had ultra-Orthodox believers, moderate believers, and total non-believers, all crowded into the compound. It was all so strange. Did we worship the same G-d as the non-believers? Who knows? But one thing was certain — we were all Jews.

Our Carpathian Jews were great believers, and placed their trust in G-d's divine promise. Many of these Jews were so ardent in their beliefs that during the Holocaust they even went to the gas-chambers believing that the Almighty would save them. Well, G-d wasn't there when the Jews were burned; so they inhaled the deadly gas fumes and perished.

I think it is also worth remembering that the pious Jews who observed the letter of G-d's law went to the gas chambers with the Shema on their lips. And the other Jews, the Zionists, the Bundists and a great many non-believers, were also there, hoping for a miracle, but it never came. Well, we in Carpathia, believed in Tchias Hameisim, and fervently hoped that the victims would find solace in Gan-Eden; but instead they were turned to ashes in Poland.

At Mateszalka, the German and Hungarian trains kept arriving and disgorging more victims. In this melee of confused humanity, I lost track of the Feldman family and alas, never saw them again. We also heard rumours that Reb Yosel's daughter Bince and her youngest daughter, Blime, had escaped into the forest, but were caught and executed by the Nazis.

We were incarcerated in Mateszalka for some two to three weeks, and then packed back into a train which traveled west across Hungary to Vienna. Then the train started speeding east through Czechoslovakia. Through the cracks in the doors we spied nameless fields, towns and

---

4   This ghetto was set up in the Jewish quarter of the city and and held around 18,000 Jews, from the locality and neighboring communities in northern Mátramaros and Szatmátr counties. Randolph L. Braham,The Politics of Genocide: The Holocaust in Hungary, Wayne State University Press, USA, 2000, p. 121

cities. We had no contact with people or communities along the way, but often when we stopped for water, a piece of bread, or a carrot or apple was thrown into the wagon by a kind person.

Once it was determined that we had entered Poland, pandemonium set in. People on the train began to recite the *Shema* and quietly mouthing the *Kaddish*. I didn't even speak to my mother—the silence said it all.

Chapter 31

The "benevolent" SS

After what seemed an eternity the train suddenly halted and the doors opened. We were blinded by the daylight. Before us was a heart-rendering scene, revealing an expanse of unimaginable human tragedy, degradation and death. This was Auschwitz.

The armed soldiers were barking unintelligible orders as we poured off the train. People either jumped or fell off. The elderly were trodden on. Everyone was crying, people being bashed and dogs were tearing people apart. If the SS intended to terrorise us into submission they succeeded beyond belief; our fears and panic were indescribable. Soon, we were forced into endless selection queues and I was separated from my mother. Families became separated, parents panicked and children screamed. I saw mothers pleading to be allowed to go with their terrified children and the "benevolent" SS, smilingly acceded to their requests. All of them went into the gas chambers. The air in Auschwitz heavy and oppressive, saturated with the stench and smoke of burning flesh. This foul air permeated our clothes, our bodies and our very souls.

In this evil industrial complex, the Nazis actually relied on young Jews to fleece their victims before driving them into the gas chambers. These dehumanised people who spoke Yiddish yelled: "*Di geist in ko-imen aran*"(You'll all go to the chimneys), as they tore the clothes off our backs. "Who are these people? Can Jews behave like that?" we queried, but our naivety and trust soon disappeared. The *mame-loshen* — the once sacred mother tongue of the Jews, for me associated with family and happy events, was being desecrated; it lost its sacredness in Auschwitz for ever.

Auschwitz existed on the principle of 'kill or be killed', and these thugs chose to kill. For six years they murdered and prostituted themselves. These youngsters traded their souls for a slice of bread, and when the war ended they disappeared into a defeated Germany, joining their Nazi brethren.

Our German-Jewish compatriots found difficulties with interpreting what was happening. Ah, they would accuse everyone other than the guilty parties. I often wondered whether this was an assimilationist attitude, or a blinding inability to see the stark realities. The crematoria burned the Jewish people, day and night, but still many German Jews maintained that the Nazis were not "cold-blooded killers."

I was of the Orthodox persuasion, so I believed that modern Zionism had brought this tragedy upon us. We bitterly denounced the Zionists for having brought this debacle upon the Jews; we never condemned the Nazis for their deeds; we saw this as a judgement from Heaven. We as a people were so used to enduring the pogroms, that we hardly uttered a word against the Holocaust.

For the Jews brought to the camps, the day of reckoning came and went: the Nazis dispatched their Holocaust accusers to the gas chambers. The tenure of office in Auschwitz was hardly ever longer than six months, and this was how millions of innocent Jews were put to death.

As I shuffled forward towards a German officer a kindly old man said to me in Yiddish "Look tall" as he threw a big oversized coat over my shoulders. This probably saved me from the gas chambers as I was terribly thin and looked about fourteen, even though I was eighteen years old.

Fortunately, after many tragic selections queues, those of us who remained were promptly despatched to trains for unknown destinations.

Chapter 32

Mauthausen to Ebensee

In early 1945, most of Eastern Europe was already in Allied hands, and the German armies tried to escape westward. As the Nazis liquidated the extermination camps in the east, they brought thousands of able-bodied inmates including me to the camps of Austria.

When we eventually alighted from the train, the mountaintop camp of Mauthausen appeared before us.[1] As the early morning May sun beamed down on us mercilessly, we were forced to run up the mountain, our legs sinking in the deep snow, biting, barking dog on all sides. We had not eaten for days and the hunger combined with the morning's heat proved devastating. If you fell you were shot. My legs quickly folded under me and I passed out. Just then Aron, a childhood

---

1   Mauthausen-Gusen concentration camp was the hub of a large group of German concentration camps that was built around the villages of Mauthausen and Sankt Georgen an der Gusen in Upper Austria, roughly 20 kilometres east of the city of Linz. The camp operated from the time of the Anschluss, when Austria was annexed into the German Third Reich in early 1938, to the beginning of May 1945, at the end of the Second World War. Starting with a single camp at Mauthausen, the complex expanded over time and by the summer of 1940 Mauthausen had become one of the largest labour camp complexes in the German-controlled part of Europe, with four main subcamps at Mauthausen and nearby Gusen, and nearly 100 other subcamps located throughout Austria and southern Germany, directed from a central office at Mauthausen.

As at other Nazi concentration camps, the inmates at Mauthausen-Gusen were forced to work as slave labour, under conditions that caused many deaths. The subcamps of the Mauthausen complex included quarries, munitions factories, mines, arms factories and plants assembling Me 262 fighter aircraft. In January 1945, the camps contained roughly 85,000 inmates. The death toll remains unknown, although most sources place it between 122,766 and 320,000 for the entire complex. Wikipedia.

friend and his father, Reb Levi Katz (Reb Yosel's son-in-law), realised that a cart was already collecting the bodies, so they quickly stood me up and between them, managed to keep me upright for the duration of the *Appell* (roll-call) I was going in and out of consciousness. Soon after this episode, hot soup was distributed and I regained my strength for the next stage of the journey.

From Mauthausen we were taken to the nearby sub camp of Ebensee[2], situated deeper in the Austrian Alps. I think Ebensee was the last bastion of Nazi resistance. It was situated high in the Alps, and while the snows had melted below by spring, up in the mountains there was plenty of it, even as late as June. By the time we got to the camp, many inmates had perished on the way. I mean, Jewish life was very cheap, and the ferocious German shepherd dogs were always close by. The war was coming to an end and we all wanted to survive, so there were no risk takers.

We were first taken to the disinfection block for delousing. Hair was cut, clothes taken, then we showered and were given camp clothes. We were assigned to a block; I remember a very long wooden hut with 3 level bunks on either side without bedding. The blocks were cleaned immaculately, forcefully. There were 90-120 men per block. Poles, Hungarians, Belgians, French, Russians and Gypsies. Each nationality grouped together and looked after its own people.

We were given potato peels in a watery broth to eat, sometimes with morsels of meat. We didn't know if it was horse meat or even human meat. We became conditioned to this meal—it didn't affect us to the extent you would think, although there was an enormous amount of diarrhea.

---

2   The Ebensee concentration camp was established by the SS to build tunnels for armaments storage near the town of Ebensee, Austria in 1943. It was part of the Mauthausen network. The construction of the Ebensee subcamp began late in 1943, and the first 1,000 prisoners arrived on November 18, 1943, from the main camp of Mauthausen and its subcamps. The main purpose of Ebensee was to provide slave labor for the construction of enormous underground tunnels in which armament works were to be housed. These tunnels were planned for the evacuated Peenemünde V-2 rocket development but, on July 6, 1944, Hitler ordered the complex converted to a tank-gear factory.
      Approximately 20,000 inmates were worked to death constructing giant tunnels in the surrounding mountains. Together with the Mauthausen subcamp of Gusen, Ebensee is considered one of the most horrific Nazi concentration camps.Wikipedia.

Although, Ebensee was comparatively small, it did not lag too far behind Auschwitz in refined brutality and dehumanisation. Many thousands of people were put to death in Ebensee without the facilities of gas chambers. There were none. Starvation, indescribable cruelty, back-breaking quarry work and the unrelenting Alpine weather all contributed to the enormous death rate. There was only one single crematorium, working day and night, without making an impact on the mountains of corpses inside and outside its perimeters. Ebensee, it seemed, was Germany's model for achieving mass exterminations on the cheap and without scientific ingenuity.

Beyond the perimeter of the camp, laughter and rejoicing could be heard from the Aryans as they frolicked in the bush. The Ebensee area was a beautiful, mountainous part of Austria, covered in a profusion of pine forests, which the population loved. Every Sunday the young people came to frolic in the woods, while the starving camp inmates were drying their bleeding wounds in the sun.

In normal circumstances, the Ebensee camp held a maximum of 8,000 inmates, but in 1945 the numbers went up to over 20,000, and they never stopped coming. The arriving inmates were terribly emaciated and starved, and perished in their hundreds.

We stopped counting the dead in the camps, and simply measured the height of the corpse piles in metres. Then after a while we referred to the dead in storeys, and it wasn't unusual to quote the height in two or three storeys. This was utterly callous, but during those terrify-ing weeks and months the piles actually represented our victory over Hitler's orderly 'civilisation.' I remember my nights were haunted by visions of degenerated humanity, of unbelievable torture and death.

When the single crematorium could no longer cope, even working day and night with three eight-hour shifts, the Nazis had us digging enormous, soul-destroying pits, in the frozen earth between the dormi-tories, in which they intended to burn the expired inmates. There the flames devoured the last vestiges of my people. Layer upon careful layer of the dead was interposed with timbers, to improve combustion. They even soaked the trench with flammable liquids in the hope that the skeletons would burn faster, but this never happened. These pits had fires burning in them, but they nurtured more smoke than flame.

Now, the stench and smoke from the decomposing bodies was reaching sons, fathers, brothers, uncles, cousins, friends and, choking them to death as well. The smouldering pits of Ebensee became a camp fixture and the smell and smoke permeated every fibre of our wretched being.

At Ebensee, Reb Levi put up a monumental struggle to survive, but the deprivation was too bad; soon his legs began to swell. Death in those desperate days was considered as a blessed relief, and it was surely a blessed relief for Reb Levi when he passed away. I had become the unofficial Block Schreiber, secretary, or record keeper, of the Jewish Hospital in Ebensee. I was very badly affected by his death, and still recall with much gratitude his untiring efforts, and those of his son Ari, in Mauthausen. Especially when they saved my life.

Ari his son became the *Stubedienst* (inmate in charge of cleaning the barracks) to the delinquent little Austrian *Blockaltester*, (elderly inmate in charge of barracks) and with my own role, this was how we both survived the Jewish Holocaust. When my dear mother passed away in 1997; Ari called —though only once —to express his condolences, and I appreciated it.

The emasculated inmates of Ebensee were forced to track twice daily through the snow-drifts, rains and heat to the distant quarries in the Alpine mountains. This, too was an integral part of the human carnage. Most of the inmates dragged their heavy swollen legs, and the Nazis delighted in making them run, literally, for their lives. The hundreds of slippery steps, which the swollen limbs had to traverse, twice daily, presented the most insurmountable obstacles. Inmates would expire along the way, but their bodies were never allowed to litter the road or, more precisely, the Alpine ecology; the living inmates had to gather up the dead and carry them back to the camp for the day's Appel (rollcall). These obsessive dawn and night musters, regardless of the Alpine weather, also contributed to the dreadful carnage. Dead or alive, the inmates had to make it to the *Appel Platz* (assembly place) to satisfy the count. After all, Hitler's credibility and that of the Third Reich depended on it.

Every day, towards nightfall, the thousands of weary Ebensee inmates would return to the *Appel Platz* from the stone quarries where they worked, and then rush in droves to the fences, to say *Kaddish* and shed tears of sorrow for those who had died. Everyone had lost someone close to them in that labyrinth of despair.

Very few inmates survived the camps unscathed. Apart from the mental anguish, there was the starvation; the beatings and the dog bites; the epidemics of internal diseases; widespread suppurating, infections and the ever-present acute frostbites. Diarrhoea and dysentery were the most persistent killer diseases and skin breaks in those swollen extremities also proved fatal. In fact, the oedema always immobilised its victims to such an extent that they lost all will to live. These poor people had to make superhuman efforts to get to the food queues and the *Appel Platz* on time. The seconds always counted - human life never did. At the musters we were often reminded that missing a count was the most criminal offence and the point was usually reinforced, by a beating or a hanging of an offender. Desperately ill inmates would make a last effort to crawl under the building foundations to find a niche in which to expire. On these occasions, the entire camp populations was detained on the *Appel Platz* for as long as it took to find the wretched victim; his punishment was public, swift and merciless.

Our German masters were compulsive record keepers and maintained the cold statistics even though the war was coming to an end. However, with the enormous influx of inmates it is doubtful that they managed to adhere to their efficiency routine, while losing the war. Consequently, it is estimated that between 12,000 and 15,000 inmates perished in Ebensee; most of them in the last weeks of the war. Even though Germany lost that war, they nevertheless derived infinite satisfaction from their successful genocidal exploits. However, when history eventually judges their deeds it must not assign all the evil credit for the Holocaust to the German people. Let us always remember that the Nazis had faithful helpers and collaborators from the occupied countries of Europe. They enthusiastically assisted the Third Reich in the Jewish Final Solution and in the violent suppression of their own people.

As I recall the horrors and exterminations of Ebensee I also remember the beautiful people of Austria frolicking in the nearby woods. While the electrified fences precluded us from joining them in the fun, we did share with them the stifling smoke from the crematorium and the burning pits. One could imagine their observations: "How well the humane Germans fed those wretched inmates. Why, they give them roasted meat dinners, everyday."

Chapter 33

A rash that saved my life

L ooking back at my own survival in Ebensee, I can only surmise that a guardian angel - in the guise of my grandma Bince
- looked after me. There, another inmate noticed a rash all
over my body and thought it was chicken pox. He told me that the
camp authorities did not tolerate infectious diseases, they dealt with
them swiftly and decisively. Was this as bad as it sounded? The next
morning I said goodbye to my friends and reported to the *Revier* - the
infirmary, where the SS doctor confirmed the chicken pox. He then
wrote on a piece of paper, gave it to me and directed me towards the
crematorium. My heart sank as I walked and I began to recite the bits
of prayers I still remembered as tears obliterated my path.

However, a little further on my spirits lifted for then I noticed an inscription in German, JEWISH INFECTIOUS BLOCK, it was located
immediately behind the crematorium. Sure enough, that's also what
my piece of paper said. I darted across the grass patch and up the long
open veranda to the office. Here, they confirmed that I was in the right
place and I felt relieved to be cheating death for a little while longer.
One quickly learned in the camp to live for the moment. This hospital
was filled beyond capacity with a range of potentially fatal diseases
and there was no medication to treat them. The patients suffering
from diphtheria, pneumonia, tuberculosis, meningitis, etc. were lying
prostrate on the bare floorboards, in so called isolation, while the less
dangerously ill occupied the crowded bunks.

The suffering in this ward was just beyond belief. Ernest, the bespectacled German *Blockaltester*, was in charge of, but certainly not responsible for this tragedy. By any standards, Ernest was a remarkably compassionate Christian inmate who felt the pain of the sick deeply, but had no medication to relieve it. He was the most humane German I had ever met.

After my rash receded I volunteered to perform some menial ward tasks. The men of the SS conducted stringent daily inspections of the hospitals and regularly selected inmates who they deemed not sick to be dispatched to the quarries and, certain death. However, they often avoided coming to the infectious block. When they did, I usually hid among the very ill inmates high on the upper bunks, and managed to survive. However, the SS often checked the hospital register, which showed admission dates, so there was no way I could stay there long term.

On my behalf Ernest had a talk with the *Blockaltester* of the non-infectious Jewish hospital. It was arranged I would transfer and work cleaning and washing. While this *Blockaltester* was not Jewish, all the orderlies and doctors in the hospital were Jewish. No medicine was administered apart from headache powder and bandages, and no surgery was performed. The most common illness was edema, swelling of the extremities. Once it started it couldn't be stopped and people drowned in their own fluids.

Since I had nice legible handwriting I was asked to design various signs, roster sheets and do other clerical as well as cleaning duties. At the front of every bunk (which usually held six to eight people) was written the name, date of birth and diagnosis of each occupant. If a patient died I was able to remove the card, note the date of death and make a duplicate of that card which I kept initially in a cupboard in the office.

In the fourteen months I was there I talked with many patients including five rabbis who volunteered valuable information about unconscious or deceased relations and friends, maybe the name of a wife or children, where they were from, and their cause of death. I took a great risk to gather all of this information, which I bundled up and covered in dirt under the floor boards. Anyone could have betrayed me for a bowl of soup or a slice of bread. They were desperate times and even decent people turned desperate. I even had accusations levelled against me, that I was getting information about the dead and their families to enrich myself after the war.

My self-imposed task of keeping records was a daunting one, because the cause of death often bore no relationship to the patient's diagnosis. Many of my fellow inmates were beaten to death, or died of malnutrition, but the stock in trade response was a denial of starvation or suffering. No one ever dared to draw attention to such things as the policy of *Vernichtung* (extermination) ; the term never even existed in the Ebensee camp. So the Nazis killed and plundered with impunity and the word *Vernichtung* never came into the equation. Even hangings, deliberate or accidental, were never listed as such. Our inmates were not 'murdered' by the thousands; they simply 'expired' or 'gave up on life' voluntarily.

The day before liberation word went out that all documents must be destroyed and the SS and their dogs went through the 28 or 29 blocks-searching for anything that anyone was keeping or hiding. During this time I was able to gather my documents, wrap them in rags and bury them under the Jewish Hospital, the last block to be searched. Around lunch time they arrived and once inside the dogs began sniffing and scratching the floor just where my bundle of records was hidden in the dirt beneath. I broke out in a cold sweat and said goodbye to a few inmates and started to recite the *Shema*—after all it was my unmistakable handwriting that would point directly to me.

Thoughts, terrifying thoughts were racing through my mind: "Will we be liberated before the dogs tear me apart or, the Nazis torture me to death?" Then, a miracle occurred, loud whistles reverberated throughout the camp and the vicious Germans and their dogs vanished. I stood there in disbelief, thanking the Almighty for having saved my life, for a third time. Later, I recovered the bundle of records and began guarding them with my life. After all, that was the price I almost paid for it.

Set in its realistic perspective, my salvaging activities of over 1,600 deceased Jewish victims in Ebensee was pitifully small. However, they were the victims who perished in that hospital during a certain time span. I envisaged that this information was going to be invaluable in remarriages, in the recital of Kaddish, in property settlements, etc., etc.

We were all ordered to gather in the *Appel Platz*. The Nazi Commandant of the Ebensee camp announced, with breaking voice that "as you have survived in the camp this long, I'm going to make sure you continue to survive. We will take you down into the quarries with food and water. You will be safest there during the final battle which is approaching."

I had some contact with the underground—two men who were working in the hospital casualty section—and they told me to spread the word that no one must go to the quarries because the plan was to blow us all up. The whispers turned to shout of defiance as twelve to fifteen thousand men learned the truth. Faced with this overwhelming determination not to move from the *Appel Platz*, the Commandant uncharacteristically backed down and we were dismissed.

The next morning we noticed that most of the camp perimeter guards were old men with World War I vintage guns. Evidently what had happened was that the SS had gone into the local village and called for volunteers "defend their town" and guard the camp to keep "the vicious criminals inside.

Talk soon started that we could easily overpower these guards with their weapons that hadn't been fired in twenty-five years. People started throwing blankets over the electric fences to insulate the current. Then someone had the good idea to turn off the electricity, and the breaking down of the fences began in earnest.

At 2.30pm on 6 May 1945 a lone black American soldier strayed into the camp, almost accidentally, and that was how Ebensee was liberated. Not having seen black skin before we all thought that he went through burning hell to get to us and, we were ecstatic. The rapport was instantaneous, but the exchanges left a lot to be desired as he spoke American English and we had no European equivalent for it. However, the emotions spoke louder than any words and they expressed it all. A short time later the rest of the G.I.'s joined the him.

Albert climbing into his bunk. "Aufsitzen" (German to "sit up")
One in a series "Thirteen Sketches from Ebensee." Artist unknown.

Capo Gustaf directing inmates. "Vorwarts" (German "forward march")
One in a series "Thirteen Sketches from Ebensee." Artist unknown.

The day of the liberation remains permanently riveted in the recesses of my mind.

While some inmates celebrated, others broke into the well stocked German stores and helped themselves, among other things, to guns and ammunition. They then went down to the town of Ebensee, got intoxicated and terrorised the Austrians who naturally claimed not to have had any inkling of the Nazi extermination camp in their midst. In the meantime, the Americans brought back captured German soldiers and put them to work in the camp. There were many incidents of retribution committed against the captured Germans, but the Americans disapproved of such violence.

I saw some of the worst offenders murdered; the Jewish Austrian Kapo of the Jewish Hospital, a little chap who was drunk all the time and very mean, the Polish Secretary of the Non-Jewish Hospital who had apparently tortured inmates before I arrived, and the tyrannical non-Jewish German Ober Kapo of all the hospitals who was close with the SS.

Our liberators supplied us generously with milk chocolates and other rich delicacies, which played havoc with stomachs unaccustomed to eating and hastened the demise of many weakened inmates. I resisted the chocolates, seeing how others were suffering and stayed with the more basic soup with meat and vegetables. Apart from general weakness as a result of malnutrition, I was dealing with a wound on my leg, an ulceration, also caused by lack of food, and I was scared that it would spread to the bone. Fortunately the medics were able to treat it and I still have my two legs.

Chapter 34

The end of the war

Germany was in tatters, and we rejoiced. Their Fatherland — Deutschland über Alles — was now destroyed. Oh, how the mighty had fallen!

The three Extermination Camps, Auschwitz, Mauthausen and Ebensee, had taught me some tragic lessons, and so I didn't risk returning heroically to Tchorna Tisa or reclaiming our lost property there. Surviving the Extermination Camps meant much more to me. I was now anxious to start a new existence, preferably as far away from Tchorna Tisa as I could make it. The Camps had taught me, beyond all else, not to play roulette with my young life but instead to savour it at all costs.

Each European country sent buses to the camps to pick up the inmates. As I had no desire to return to Zakarpatska Ukraina, I chose the capital of Czechoslovakia, Prague to start my new life. Unfortunately I had to wait at the camp for two weeks after the war ended. Then the Czech buses arrived in Ebensee to pick us up and on the way, we passed through Hitler's Germany, where the destruction was complete.

When we arrived in Prague in 1945 we were liberated Holocaust survivors, and the Czech people made us very welcome. Our reception in Prague was something else. We arrived on trucks from Ebensee and were unloaded on Vaclavske Namesti, which was filled to capacity. People standing 20 deep welcomed our return.

The people of Prague had taken up every vantage point. The balconies were full, and the trees and rooftops sagged under their weight. The cheering never stopped. The tears flowed freely on both sides, and the people were so friendly and excited that it made me cry once again. Here at last were the bedraggled victims of the Nazi Holocaust, and the City of Prague was celebrating our return.

Until this very moment we had no idea of the kind of reception the Jews would get in Prague, but we need not have worried. The Czech people were more generous than I could ever have imagined. We were dragged in all directions and plied with food as the people shared their meagre rations with us. All of this happened about 60 years ago, but I can still see it as if it were yesterday. I would not trade those memories for anything.

Flickering little candles burned all over the streets of Prague. They commemorated the precious lives of the resistance movement. Judging by the profusion of lights, those battles must have raged throughout the city. People even brought flowers and colourful ribbons to commemorate the lives of their dear ones.

Among the flowers were small, endearing messages of love, and every time I passed them tears of gratitude rolled down my face. This was a sight to behold. The Czech people certainly laid down their precious lives so that we might all live in peace! What a wonderful privilege it was to experience this!

I was pleased that none of the blood had been wiped away yet, and we could see the intensity of the battles. At sundown the people of Prague gathered around the splattered spots of blood, to pay homage to the lives lost. Oh, they wept bitterly for their loved ones, but the tears could not bring them back. There were bloody spots everywhere, and I was so glad that I could still see them. People just stopped to say their prayers, and that was the most satisfying sight of all.

At long last, it was no crime to be a Jew, and the people in Prague never even asked our nationalities; we were all Czechs. I have never experienced such hospitality in all my life.

In Prague I learned that the Nazis had taken away everything they could lay their hands on, but they still did not stifle the spirit and goodness of the Czech people. The Czechs had withstood the years of tyranny, and lived to see the safe return of the survivors in 1945. I still recall the processions of trucks arriving from the extermination camps: cargoes of human skeletons. The Czechs cheered themselves hoarse each time, and I will always remember their unstinting generosity in their greeting. The Czechs shared all they had, lavishing it upon us all. I was never asked who I was, and nobody wanted to know my nationality. They made no distinction between the different survivors of the Holocaust; we were all returners from hell.

The workers of the *Catholic Charita* of Prague were there in full force, and their kindness was indescribable. They clothed our emaciated bodies and found accommodation and employment for all who wanted it. We camp people were emaciated and needed hospitalisation, food, clothing, and a kind word, and the churches provide it all. They simply established nourishing centres, medical and hospital care and asked nothing in return.

Special hospitals were set up to deal with the influx of returnees, and people with tuberculosis were sent straight to the sanatoria. Even I was dispatched to a villa in the country, where I recuperated for ten days.

Although I was very thin, my health was in reasonable shape and so they placed me in a Jewish orphanage in Belgicka Street in the suburb of Vinohrady.

During my time in Prague, I was able to devote time to sorting through my prized camp hospital records. I produced alphabetical lists and forwarded them to the United Nations Secretariat, and the Jewish World Congress in London. The original documentation was neatly arranged in a filing cabinet, which I was going to deposit, in due course, at *Yad Vashem*. the world centre for holocaust research, documentation, education and commemoration. I felt that the holy city of Jerusalem, was the most fitting resting place for the tormented souls whose lives were so cruelly extinguished in the Holocaust.

Chapter 35

Prague city life

The Belgicka orphanage became a popular venue for young people, who made illegal departures to Palestine from here. This meant that the Belgicka was filled to capacity every night; then by morning most of the young people had disappeared. Only the regulars remained in the orphanage.

Usually the German border was the crossing point. This was the site of a trade in human cargo, which extended across the whole of Europe, and the Belgicka was a staging point. Even the European Governments were anxious to co-operate in this illegal trade, as long as they were assured of silence about their own Nazi collaborations. The Zionists were only too happy to oblige: they were building a Jewish Homeland, and needed this illegal movement of the masses.

In the orphanage, we lived in dormitory accommodation and were given basic sustenance. The Charita augmented our needs with food coupons and clothing without ever asking our religion, simply viewing us as Holocaust survivors in need. I will never forget this!

The Charita strived to be both non-denominational and impartial; it simply portioned out generous helpings of human kindness. Since they never knocked back anyone who asked for help, this gave rise to incidents of cheating and lying. The clean, charitable Charita provided magnificent potential for some unscrupulous

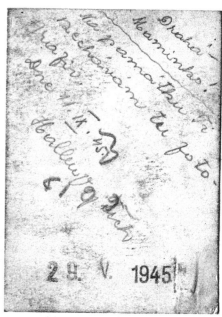

survivors, who would receive free clothing from the Charita, and then go to the flea markets and sell them.

The workers found it difficult to believe that their charity was being abused or squandered like this. Alas, some of my Holocaust colleagues were experts in both cheating and lying; they had to be, to survive in the camps. So they lined up for extra portions of bread, soup, warm jackets or anything else that was going. Then they traded (or sold) all these things they got for nothing, on the black market. I remember they fronted up with all sorts of dubious excuses to obtain more items.

Soon the word had spread that Prague was an easy target, and so it became the focal point for all kinds of deals, which the Czechs called shmelina. In fact this became so easy that Prague graduated to become the smuggling capital of Europe, and the Belgicka orphanage was the unofficial headquarters. There, people simply arrived at night and were gone before dawn. Nobody asked for any travel documents, and the nights in the Belgicka turned into a time of shmelina and clandestine activities. In the postwar years there was turmoil everywhere, and the Holocaust survivors believed they owed loyalty to no one. So they simply arrived after sunset, slept for a few hours and left before dawn, doubtlessly believing that the world owed them a living.

Then there were other groups moving across national borders, and they turned their deceptions into an art form. They were the undisputed specialists, whom the Czech police called black-marketeers. These were Holocaust survivors aiming for bigger things than a piece of bread or a bowl of soup. They traded in truckloads of hard-to-get things, like cigarettes and alcohol. National borders were there for the mugs, not for the highly trained smugglers, who lived above the law. They knew how to silence border guards and smuggle goods without licenses.

The situation became so bad that if a crime was committed in Prague the police would immediately pursue the Holocaust survivors —they were known as the trained experts in criminal deception, and this sullied all our reputations. At one stage it became so bad that I was even ashamed to admit to being a Holocaust survivor.

On the one side of the border was a defeated Germany and on the other a Germany divided into four zones — American, Russian, English and French. The Western Powers cleverly combined their authority against the Soviet zone, and this suited the black-marketeers quite admirably. They always favoured the American Zone, which had an inexhaustible supply of everything; so the black-marketeers simply backed up their vehicles and loaded them up to the hilt. Then crossing the borders presented no difficulties; all the guards were also on the payroll. Now if a border guard was ever unbribable, then the Holocaust immunity always won the day. The authorities did not know how to deal with the menace. No authority in its right mind would ever prosecute a Holocaust survivor for trying to make a living. These young thugs learned their trade in the Holocaust, and deceiving the Nazis was also a piece of cake. Even the French, English and American guards were bamboozled by their explanations; they were Nazi trained smugglers par excellence!

Even military trucks were often stolen and sold on the open market. However, I had no aptitude for these shady deals, nor was I willing to pursue them. At this stage I was barely 20 years old, and a Holocaust survivor without a trade. While I was regaining my strength, I discovered that there was a training position for me at the Tesla works, but not in the middle of the year. In the meantime, the Belgicka orphanage was full, and so I was transferred to the Krakovska Home, which was

not far from the Narodni Divadlo (The National Theatre) on Vaclavske
Namesti.

Mother and son, Prague 1946.

While at the Krakovska Home, I had a most pleasant surprise. Upon
returning there one evening, I found mother, hail and hearty, sitting
in the dormitory. It was a happy and tearful reunion tinged with sadness and disappointment. She told me that after our separation in
Auschwitz she was sent to Buchenwald. After her liberation she went
back to Jasina and after finding no family survivors there, came to
Prague. My mother had acquired a fully furnished two-bedroom flat in
Usti-nad-Labem. This was a Czech border district, from which all the
German owners were expatriated to Germany and their abodes given
to Holocaust survivors.

I was naturally delighted to have my mother back, but was somehow loath to return to the unhappy relationship we both endured in Yasina. She has always been a domineering personality, with a flaring temper, and I now craved independence and a modicum of adult assertiveness. Of course, my mother assumed that I would come back and live there happily ever after. But I already had made other plans for my future and, poor mum returned home to Usti nad Labem empty handed. So I stayed in Prague, and divulged to no one that my mother had a flat in Usti-nad-Labem. After I left Czechoslovakia, mother migrated to Israel, but we have kept in close touch over the years.

The supervisor of the Krakovska Home, a woman, also hailed from Jasina , and so we soon established a fabulous rapport. Because I had a few months to spare until my training position started, I got myself a nine-to-five job at the Narodni Sprava Majetkovych Podstat (NSMP). The NSMP was not that far away from the headquarters of the Jewish Community, in Maislova Ulice.

The NSMP was a government instrumentality, engaged in recouping Jewish properties from the mischlings; these were Germans who had married Czech girls. The NSMP was administered by Jews, but it presented a few uncharitable problems. You see, the properties to be repossessed were often enormous, and the surviving claimants rather few, so this opened up a Pandora's Box. People cheated left, right and centre, with lucrative opportunities opening up for the unscrupulous operators, and the NSMP became embroiled in enormous embezzlements.

In our department, apart from Mr Zucker, there were also Mr Stepan Kisch, Mrs Jindra Horackova, a young typist and yours truly. This was my first job after the Holocaust, and it was fabulously creative. I mean, working with these innovative people was a real privilege, and it gave me a new perspective on life. All of them were very kind and helpful, at a time when I most needed kindness in order to regain my confidence in humanity. You see, the extermination camps had left me with some very weird ideas about human beings, and I had to be convinced that there was still honesty and integrity in this world.

Our department wasn't exactly the ideal place for this sort of education, however, because the people we dealt with were invariably suspects. Vilem Zucker's task was to investigate fraud, embezzlement and other criminal activities perpetrated against Jewish properties. The Nazis had often given treasured items to their cronies as a form of bribery, to keep them in the National Socialist fold. A lot of this went on, and then after the war the NSMP had to find the bona fide owners of these treasured items, and return them.

So Zucker's investigative division was responsible to the highest authority in the land—the Government of Czechoslovakia. We had the task of auditing the other departments and ferreting out the deceptions in those departments, and making sure that the pilferers didn't dispose of the properties before we got to them. Consequently, our department had the privileged designation of I/1, signifying that it investigated all misappropriation in the organisation. Then, because of its investigative nature, I soon discovered that it was more appropriate not to divulge my section, and once I learned this, the bulk of the hostilities were subdued. I remember that one department head pilfered things incessantly; then he developed lung cancer, and I hoped that the disease would save him from punishment, but it didn't. He was sentenced, and died in prison.

When the prosecutions intensified, I was even more reluctant to divulge my place of employment. Mind you, I had nothing to do with the pilfering or the prosecutions, but being employed by the organisation did taint me with the same brush. My duties had nothing to do with pilfering, however. I was the chief designer of forms for the entire organisation, but the guilt by association principle caused me to be included in the investigative circle.

My boss, Vilem Zucker, was a fabulous fellow; his copious grey head of hair was the talk of the town; he always brushed it right back to disclose a kindly face and a ready smile. I enjoyed his generous repository of down-to-earth wisdom and level-headed judgements. In different circumstances, he would have been a mathematical genius; he always mulled over insurmountable, complex equations, maintaining that high mathematics calmed his nerves and aided him in resolving "insoluble problems." Well, I certainly had no arguments against this logic, and always considered him to be a brilliant mathematician and philosopher who employed algebraic formulae to resolve human failings.

But, if the truth be known, though I was supposed to act creatively rather than mathematically, I often wished I had half of Mr Zucker's intelligence. The office never gave me any title, but I planned and designed forms for the whole organisation. I wish they would have paid me the appropriate rate. Anyway, the departments submitted outlines of their forms to me and I drew them up accordingly, and then returned them for comments. Often they came back to be redesigned, and I passed them on to the printing office. In other words, I was the indispensable intermediary between the organisation and the printing department. But if I had problems with any design, Vilem Zucker's door was always open to me.

Actually, I had an excellent relationship with all my superiors and in the process, discovered that Stepan Kisch was the cousin of that other Kisch, the philosopher, who jumped ship in Sydney and was duly imprisoned. Although we admired each other immensely, none of us ever dared to use first names, and I was always known to my colleagues as Halmicku, an endearment I still value. Jindra Horackova was also a dear colleague of mine whom I admired very much. Mrs Horackova dealt with matters on a higher plane and was often the sounding board for both Mr Zucker and Mr Kisch. Finally, the only other person in that office was the young typist, with whom I used to smooch; but no other pleasurable relationships ensued.

I lined up a radio-mechanic's apprenticeship with the Tesla Radio works in Prague, to commence at the start of 1948. I was twenty-two years of age, and already seven years over the apprenticeship period, so my opportunities were shrinking by the day. Who would employ a twenty-two-year-old apprentice, I wondered. Would I forever remain a side-kick? A best man, but never the groom?

To accept an apprenticeship with Tesla Radio, I had to resign from my current job. The apprenticeship was going to last three years, but the political situation in Europe was now rapidly deteriorating.

The enjoyment I derived from living in Prague was marred by the festering Holocaust wounds, which refused to heal. Somehow I had to escape the tragic past. Moving to another European country was not the solution but, perhaps, migrating to the ends of the earth, I felt, would help to heal the wounds. I made some inquires and to my surprise, found an opportunity to migrate to Australia. I knew nothing about the continent or its people, but the fact that it was so far removed from Germany, suited me fine. I contacted a Mrs Anita Freiberger-ova, in the OSE office, who promised to make all the travel arrangements for me.

I registered at the Jewish Communal Centre, in Meislova Ulice in a slightly clandestine fashion because there were two underlying problems—I was of age for military service in Czechoslovakia, and I had no trade. In the application my age was reduced to seventeen, so I would be too young for the military and young enough to be considered an eligible Australian migrant. In Australia, the apprenticeships were five years long. I was already twenty, and with the best will in the world I would still have been twenty-five when my apprenticeship finished. Although Australia had no compulsory military service, they made it up with a five-year apprenticeship. There kids finished their schooling at fifteen and had a trade by twenty.

Living in Prague, I was always keeping my ears to the ground for any possibilities of departing troublesome Europe forever. As far as I was concerned, Germany — divided or united — still remained the most potent destructive force on the Continent. I simply had to get away, and put as much distance between Europe and myself as I could. It was already clear to me that the Western powers were resurrecting Germany as a bulwark against Communism. But the nations on the other side of the divide were doing the same thing. In other words, the world was being inexorably driven into a third World War.

In the aftermath of World War II, the ardent Nazi warriors were shedding their distinctive uniforms and making every conceivable effort to get to the American, English or French zones of Germany. They knew that the Nazi past was not going to awaken a great deal of interest there. Although many Nazis claimed vague anti-Nazi affiliations, it seemed that there were no Nazis in postwar Germany. They all managed to fabricate new, outlandish identities, and even Hitler himself was disowned in his own land.

The West was no longer interested in the past, but more concerned with the here and now. Germany had been defeated, but International Communism was now on the rise, so the West began training its former enemy Germany against its former ally Russia. It was Stalin's evil Communism that was gaining ground everywhere. Now the German forces had to be reorganised in a hurry.

The Americans were convinced that, the more dedicated the Germans had been to the Nazi cause, the greater their devotion would be to the forthcoming battles. But although the cold war was in full swing, the nations who had fought Hitler were so depleted and so impoverished that another war seemed to be out of the question. President Truman and his ilk put in place the Marshall Plan to resurrect West Germany. So the conquered nation was enjoying a revival while the rest of Europe starved. I still remember how the Czech people struggled to survive while the Germans, across the border, wallowed in luxuries even as they lived amongst war-torn buildings. As a Jewish Holocaust Survivor, this sudden change of heart did not sit well with me at all. My enemies were, first and foremost, the Nazis who had brought Hitler to power and declared war on the Jewish people. These feelings left no room for any crafty manipulations; I simply could not accept my sworn enemies as allies in this new war of expediency.

In the meantime, I left my NSMP job and became an apprentice with the "Tesla" radio factory. Before long the time of departure arrived and, owing to the prevailing political instability, I was instructed to leave everything behind and dramatically disappear, without any explanations or goodbyes (except to my mother.)

Though I heard stories of untamed Aborigines roaming the streets of Sydney and Melbourne, I reasoned that they couldn't possibly be worse than the civilised Germans of Europe. So I quickly informed my mother of my plans and since the Czech government intended to seal its borders, she made urgent arrangements herself to go to Israel. In this way, she hoped we might even see each other occasionally. Well, it all worked in our favour, and I visited Israel quite regularly and sent her food parcels to sustain her.

My greatest regret was leaving my country of birth and the kindness of its people. However, a new life was beckoning and I had to give myself a chance to rise above the past and start afresh. I boarded the train to Paris and bid goodbye to Czechoslovakia.

Chapter 36

Going to Australia

The Parisian arrival in 1947 was less than auspicious. The French people did not have the warmth, compassion or the humanity of the Czech; they were positively hostile and very arrogant. Postwar rationing was still in full swing and our group had no entitlements and no claims to be fed. We were undesirable intruders poaching the little food France had for its citizens. The Jewish relief organisations accommodated us in the palatial *Fonteney aux Roses* - an orphanage, which had seen better days. Food here was also extremely scarce, but a guardian angel named Rita Leistner, tried gallantly to make us forget our hunger pains. She managed to fill the recesses of our bellies with matters cultural, which abounded in Paris. Meanwhile, France was crippled by general strikes and no buses were available to take us to the docks in the port of Marseille. It wasn't till two months later that buses were made available for our journey. However, when they disgorged the passengers the empty vehicles were set alight.

Meanwhile, the waiting boat in Marseille harbour was a wreck named *SS Teti*. She miraculously delivered us to Haifa, in Palestine. We arrived here without realising that in the excitement our luggage was forgotten and, it never reappeared. If the French situation was potentially dangerous the position in Palestine was positively explosive.

I recall being on Haifa's Mount towards the end of 1947, when the War of Liberation was fought. The poor Jews had the British on the one side, and the Arabs on the other, while the nightly skirmishes continued unabated. In the meantime, a sizeable group of young survivors including me, was stranded on Mount Carmel, deliberating whether to fight with their brethren or demand a passage on the high seas. In my case I was looking for stability and to get as far away from war as possible.

Food was scarce, we had no luggage and intermittent shooting went on day and night. During the two months we were stranded there some of us managed to find work through the courtesy of local taxi drivers who would pick up labourers along the streets and deliver us to various employers. The drivers were also responsible for collecting our pay packets, but somehow those weighty envelopes got lost in transit; we never saw them. Nice people those Palestinian taxi drivers, just do not trust them with any pay packets!

Eventually we got word that a ship bound for Australia would soon dock. The life on this ship, the *SS Partizanka* was sheer luxury. There was plenty of food and clandestine romance also flourished between the Jewish boys and the Greek maidens on board.

The journey took some three weeks and we arrived in Fremantle to a generous kosher luncheon and a few gifts. In the afternoon we re-boarded the ship and headed for Melbourne. Here, we disembarked to a distinctly subdued Jewish reception and caught an overnight sleeper to Sydney.

It was a hot February morning when we arrived and Sydney's sponsoring organisations, the Australian Jewish Welfare Society and the Australian Welfare Guardian Society were out there in force. Their warmth was overwhelming and we were taken to a communal reception in the Maccabean Hall.

There, immediate relationships were being forged with our hosts by gesticulations and sign language; none of the arrivals spoke any English. After an exhaustive day of pleasantries, some of us were taken to Hunters Hill's Isabella Lazarus Home for Jewish Children. There, we had a ready-made English teacher in Mr Schneider who was of

Hungarian extraction while the resident Chef catering for our culinary needs was a Greek. The kind Chef only had one item on the menu; and steak and eggs for breakfast, lunch and dinner. A good wholesome diet, which never varied. I got so used to steak and eggs that for months after I left the home, I didn't know how to chose anything else. However, as soon as my English improved sufficiently I promptly stopped eating meat for quite a while after.

Once I was settled I dispatched an urgent letter to Vilem Zucker and the entire department I had left behind, thanking them all for their kindness, and received a very suitable reply from Jindra Horackova. However, that was over fifty years ago, and I am sure that all my dearest friends are now picking daisies in the never never; I am looking forward to meeting them all in the great beyond.

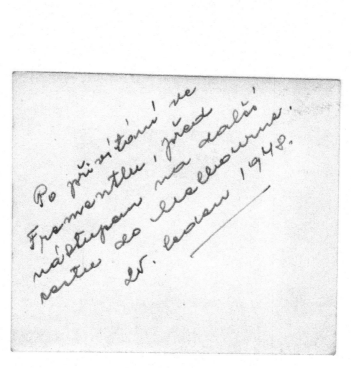

Albert's handwriting

In Fremantle, Western Australia, 1948. Jewish communal welcome lunch. Albert arrowed on right.

Sydney, circa 1953

Chapter 37

Life in Australia

On weekends we all deserted our Hunters Hill haven for the Shabbat hospitality in private homes. There, we eagerly practiced our English vocabulary and enjoyed the culinary changes. I was fortunate in having formed an early bond with Mr and Mrs Sydney D. Einfeld and my weekends were spent, pleasurably, in their home at 162 Military Road, Dover Heights. Both Billie and Syd Einfeld together with their children Marcus and Robyn, accepted me graciously into their home and family, as a son and brother. Later my wife Ruthie and our children, Peter and Bonita were also welcomed into the Einfeld clan. Our unique and warm relationship with the Einfelds has continued to flourish and we hope and pray that it may continue.

In Sydney, I befriended three Aboriginal sisters. They were servant girls in different households, but often disappeared for two or three weeks at a time. Then, without as much as How do you do, they reappeared. They were itinerant workers, pitch black in appearance, with exaggerated noses, more closely resembling the African nomads than the Australian Aborigines. However, I was heartened that the Aborigines also sought land rights and recognition. We are all entitled to a little place in the sun, regardless of our colour or creed.

Although I studied English assiduously in the Maccabean Hall, I still could not understand the Aussies, nor could they understand me.

However, I did notice the politeness in the streets, and began carrying my English dictionary with me. But it wasn't helpful; time and again I failed to translate the spoken words. Even *Gesindheit* wasn't in the dictionary, and Bless You was still a novelty to me. I was rather surprised about the popularity of that expression. However, I was very impressed when, on my first day in Elizabeth Street, I sneezed and a complete stranger said *Bless You*. Little did he know that I couldn't even understand him — but that didn't matter. I found that while the people here were still obsessed with bush-rangers and convicts, this was slowly disappearing, and the locals were friendly and charming.

I was overflowing with gratitude, and I smiled at all and sundry. I even focused my attention on total strangers in the street, and encountered a few unexpected smiles. Those lingering smiles scored friendship points, and the sour looks earned demerits. You see, my European background trained me to evaluate facial features. Even the *Bless You* expression acquired a meaning for me. People were sullen in Europe and friendliness did not come easily to them. So seeing friendliness in Australia was reassuring and very satisfying. I am glad I came here, to feel hale and hearty in a new land, among friendly people.

After arriving in Australia, I was anxious to continue my Radio Trades Course. At the Petersham Technical College my new classmates were barely sixteen while I was a non-English speaking twenty-three year old. Furthermore, they enjoyed the comfort and convenience of home and the material support of their parents while I had no such luxuries. My sponsoring Jewish Welfare Society would have been also far happier had I chosen a factory job, and began earning some money, rather than tenaciously resisting their advice. I knew it was not going to be easy, but I was determined to become a tradesman, regardless of the obstacles.

I struggled with my class work but in time, began showing steady progress. My assignments also sounded progressively more English and the exam results became very creditable. I managed to maintain a position among the three top students right through the duration of the course. At the final Graduation Night in 1953, I was called to the podium of the Leichhardt Town Hall, to receive the "A" grade prize in the Radio Trades Course. Billie and Syd Einfeld were there for me to share in my joyful achievement. My five year traineeship was served with the Radio Centre at Kings Cross, and I was indebted to the Edel brothers for the opportunity. In time, I also managed to repay the outlay that the Welfare Society expended on me. I feel that achieving the Certified Tradesman's status certainly vindicated my stubborn determination.

The elation of becoming a tradesman did not last very long. I suddenly became aware that most traders in my field dealt in German manufactured goods. Australian products were disappearing off the shelves and Polydor records and Telefunken sets took their place. Dealing in German manufactured goods so soon after the Holocaust was a festering sore in my heart. I had learned a trade for five years and subsequently acquired a managerial position. But finding myself promoting and selling German products while wrestling with my conscience as a Holocaust survivor was too much. In the end my integrity was at stake and I could not reconcile the two positions; I had to resign.

It seemed that the only respectable occupation for a former Holocaust survivor was in the treatment or caring fields. I lacked the entree qualifications for medicine and was not particularly interested in a nursing career.

However, inquiries showed that there were ancillary professions such as Diagnostic Radiography that would suit me well. This was a three year part-time course, which again required serving a accredited hospital traineeship. Not having found a hospital to employ me I persuaded the course authorities to allow me to proceed with the first two years of the curriculum. This gave me some breathing space and time to find a position. Ultimately, Sydney Hospital's Bob Bailey relented and offered me employment in the final year. I graduated in Medical Radiography, in 1957, and soon after was transferred to the Prince of Wales Hospital (POWH).

My perseverance did pay off, and I found my rewards in helping to diagnose the sick — an infinitely more rewarding experience than repairing German electrical goods.

In time, POWH became the accredited Principal Teaching Hospital of the University of New South Wales and I, its Chief Radiographer. My

career in Medical Radiography spanned over a period of thirty-five
years and I retired as Departmental Manager, in August 1990.

Sydney Hospital, circa 1957

In my long career I served on the NSW Australian Institute of Radiography (AIR) and was, for a time, on the panel of examiners for the
professional Fellowship. I also had an input at State and Federal levels
in matters of Radiation Protection and my expertise was often sought
in judicial inquiries. In education, I was a Radiography lecturer and
examiner, for over twenty-five years and saw many hundreds of gradu-
ates enter the profession and make a worthwhile contribution to the
health of the nation.

My work in the hospital presented many opportunities to undertake
and participate in research and write and present diagnostic papers at
professional conferences. Thus, on the International scene I presented
papers at conferences in Madrid, Brussels, Antwerp, London, Paris,
Kingston, Montreal and Las Vegas. In Australia, I also presented a
great many papers at national technical conferences annually and have
won the coveted Philips-Stanford Award for excellence in 1967 and
again in 1971. In 1967 I also had the honour of being the NSW James
N. Young Memorial Orator.

However, the most cherished attainments in my career are the Fellowship of the Australian Institute of Radiography in 1967, and the Order of Australia Medal for Medicine, especially Radiography in 1983.

While working in a part-time capacity at Edels in 1955 I had the good fortune of meeting there my future wife, Ruth Denoff. We were married on 20 May 1956 at the Great Synagogue. Ours was and is a blissful and blessed marriage nurtured by mutual affection and respect.

We are also the proud parents of son Peter Everett and, daughter Bonita. Both our children reside in Los Angeles and are particularly well adjusted individuals and successful in their respective fields of endeavour. Peter and his lovely wife, Pascale, have at last made us proud grandparents with their beautiful India Ashley, born on 21 August 1995.

Ruth has pursued a lifelong interest in singing and theatrical work while I devoted my energies to communal and professional pursuits. To mention but a few of the communal involvements, I was President of the Kingsford-Maroubra Hebrew Congregation between 1978 and 1982. My sustained involvement in the work of the Synagogue was acknowledged in 1992, with a Life Vice Presidency.

In 1981, I attended the inspirational World Gathering of Holocaust Survivors, in Jerusalem. Thereafter, I returned to Sydney with the idea of creating a representative body that would allow Survivors to have a local voice. The Australian Association of Jewish Holocaust Survivors (AAJHS) came into being and I became its founding President. The Jerusalem Gathering also inspired the idea of a reunion of Survivors in Australia, and in 1985, the fortieth anniversary of the demise of Nazi Germany we staged the very successful International Gathering of Holocaust Survivors, at the University of N.S.W. in Sydney.

Attendance far exceeded our expectations and it was heartening to see so many young people including my own kids at the lectures and participating in the discussions. Peter and Bonita came home and said "Dad why didn't you tell us this?" During their childhood, they knew I was a survivor but I hadn't wanted to place my burden on their shoulders. I was rather pleased that they were able to learn my story in the framework of the Gathering.

In 1989 I authored *The Gift Of Life*, a commemorative book which enshrined for posterity the brilliant papers presented at this first Sydney Holocaust Gathering.

Albert speaking at a wreath laying ceremony for fallen liberators of the concentration camps, Sydney 1985. Photo: Australian Association of Jewish Holocaust Survivors

Part VI

Connecting with the past

Chapter 38

Searching for relatives

The Holocaust had decimated my large family in Jasina, and I felt now was the time to reach out and somehow bring together the remnants. I became zealous in my search, and letters of enquiry went out far and wide. I was now reaching my 70th birthday, and when one is this age G-d only knows how many more years an individual has on this Earth; time was short, but I enjoyed the search.

It's interesting how things start. In 1993, I started researching and compiling ideas for this book, but, as everyone knows, the task of writing an autobiography takes an inordinate amount of time. I decided to visit my mother in Israel to discover more about the family. She was a wealth of information and directed me to contact my cousins Chaya and Goldi. They were the children of Urtze (Favish) Berger and his wife Rachel Halm,[3] one of three Jewish families who lived at the Behensky bridge, near the Katz family; in whose house we used to pray on Shabbes. Unfortunately, none of the parents survived the Holocaust. But Rachel's daughters, Goldi and Chaya, returned from the Holocaust.

They both live in Mazor, Israel, almost across the street from each other. I found Goldi rather distant, but Chaya was infinitely friendlier, and bedded me down in her lounge room for a night or two. Chaya and

---

3   Rachel was the daughter of Moishe Halm and Golde Goldenberg. Moishe was the son of our original ancestors in Tchorna Tisa Avrom Dovid and Sure-Yente Halm. It's interesting to note that Moishe's sister Yitte (Rose) Halm married Golde Goldenberg's brother Srool Avrom, so we were connected to the Goldenberg branch of the family by two marriages.

I actually corresponded for a while, and then it all petered out. However they gave me names and addresses of many long lost relatives in the USA.

I also arranged to visit cousin Klari (Chaya) Berman, who lived in Haifa. I wanted to relive the memories of her flamboyant father, Yidde Tessler, my mother's half brother.[4] That shiny motorbike in the photograph, which I still remembered, conjured up romantic escapades for me. I had never met my cousin Klari and didn't know her age but, I believed that at 68 years of age I myself should make the effort. After all, I thought, how long are we likely to remain on this Earth and be mobile enough to see the world?

Well, when I arrived, Cousin Klari was waiting for me in the street. She introduced herself, and then, because her unit was not easy to find, she guided me to her door. When we walked inside there was an enormously attractive vista in front of us overlooking Haifa. Her lounge room was modestly furnished. Did she live there on her own? Was she separated or divorced? A great many questions crowded my mind, but I didn't ask any of them as Cousin Klari seemed a very private person. During the hour I spent with her she did provide me with a good deal of background information for my autobiography.

She was kind enough to lend me some family photographs, which I had copies made of in the USA, and duly returned them to her. I don't know why, when I was looking forward to meeting the daughter of my uncle, I was expecting her to be as extroverted as her father. Mind you, I only imagined him to be an extrovert for I never actually met him as he had moved to Romania before my time. Anyway, the silences with Klari were long, and pregnant with expectations that were never realized. She was refined, reserved and somehow totally detached; She showed no interest in any other member of our family, and didn't even inquire about her father's living sister, my mother Nelly, living in Beersheva.

However, Klari did give me Rita Kaminsky's address in Florida, USA. Rita is Klari's cousin, and daughter of Yidde's sister Dori. Anyway, I

---

4   Yidde (Eugene) Tessler was a son of Avrom Wolf Eisikovits and Chaya Tessler, born prior to my great grandmother Bince marrying Avrom Wolf. So he was my mother Nelly's half brother.

was delighted to have this contact in the USA and quickly dispatched an inquisitive letter. I remember that her response brought tears to my eyes. Here were two strangers, in their sixties, with the only commonality being a tenuous span reaching out beyond their years: Rita's grandfather was also my grandfather, Avrom Wolf.

After Israel in 1993 we visited our children, Peter and Bonita, in Los Angeles, and excitedly made contact with my long lost cousin Rita Kaminsky, in Florida. Rita readily accepted my telephone call from Los Angeles — the excitement was very much reciprocated. This enthusiasm augured well for the future and I expected a dynamic run of correspondence, but it never eventuated. I was the sentimental one in this relationship, feeling that we had already lost an inordinate amount of time in inexplicable silence.

I kept writing and writing, but my letters went unanswered for 18 months or more, and then finally I received a reply. The information enlightened me about aunt Dori's life, and I now had references to her extended family in the USA. My mother did have old photographs of her half-sister and husband, but I was rather moved that Dori's daughter was sharing some of her mother's life with a relative she did not know. In the letter was a copy of her mother's original travel document, dated 21 July 1921 — four years before I was even born. This document entitled Aunt Dori to depart from Jasina through Germany and Holland and ultimately land in the USA. At the time, Dori was 23 years of age, and two years later she married Jack Galka. It seems that they were rather active, for during the next five years they produced three children —Paul, Roslyn and Rita.

Cousin Rita was also kind enough to give me an important cameo of Dori's life, for which I am most grateful. She portrayed her mother as, "A warm-hearted and intelligent lady with a refreshing sense of humour who passed away in 1956, after just one heart attack". Cousin Rita's mother was 59 years of age when she died, and two years later her father passed away as well. Then in 1989 cousin Rita was widowed.

In her correspondence, Cousin Rita also supplied me with information about our aunt Adele. The two sisters arrived in the USA in the early 1920s, and Adele married a William Greenberg and they made their home in New York. This marriage produced three children named Maurice (Moe), Claire and Julius, but according to Rita none of them are alive. Rita assured me that their six descendants are still alive, but she had lost contact with them all.

After this sojourn, I went to visit Hersh Einhorn[1], another cousin from Tchorna Tisa, who now resides in Kiriyat Bialik, near Haifa. Hersh is married to Miriam, and they have a son and daughter who also live nearby with their families. Many, many decades ago, Hersh was a neighbour of ours in Tchorna Tisa, and when I met up with him again I was overcome by the warmth and hospitality of he and his family.

I also managed to find out the whereabouts of my old neighbours and cousins, the Katz's.[2] With the war over, Charlotte had gone to Sweden to recuperate, and met her husband David Lenga there. Cila went to the USA and later Israel. Yoli migrated to Israel, and Ari settled in Montreal, Canada. There was yet another sister, Blima, the youngest, but she and her parents never survived the Holocaust. I made a point of getting together with Cila Wald and Yoli Urnoi when I was in Israel. They were most welcoming and very hospitable.

On our 1995 trip to Los Angeles to see our own children Peter and Bonita, we made a point of seeing Charlotte and David Lenga. Back in Tchorna Tisa my relationship was closest with cousin Ari. When we were all taken away to Auschwitz we lost touch with the girls but Ari and their father Levi Katz were with me in Mauthausen and Ebensee. I have never forgotten how Levi and Ari saved my life in Mauthausen. Alas, after many weeks of suffering Levi passed away in Ebensee.

However, all four Katz offspring kept in touch with each other, and we can only hope that their children will do the same. In Tchorna Tisa we had seen each other practically every day, because the Katz abode was on my way to school. I also recall the wonderful times we all had in

---

1   Hersh was the son of Benzin Halm and Chana Einhorn, and grandson of Yitte (Rose) Halm and Srool Avrom Goldenberg.

2   Cila, Yoli, Ari and Charlotte Katz were the children of Levi Katz and Bince Jahr who lived in the house used as our local synagogue by the Behensky Bridge. Bince, and her sisters Feige, Sure-Yente and brother Mendl Jahr were the offspring of Yosel Halm and Silke Jahr who were our neighbors in Tchorna Tisa. Yosel was a son of Avrom Dovid and Sure-Yente Halm and Silke was the brother of Kalmen Jahr.

the fields of Tchorna Tisa, when we bedded down at night to guard the hay.

In the meantime, back in Sydney we received a call from Eddy Gandler who divulged that we were related, and from then on many things began falling into place. You see, Eddy was the son of Bleema Halm[3] and Eddy's son Larry fell in love with a girl from Melbourne, and they eventually married. The young Gandlers settled in Melbourne and the American Gandlers all came up to Sydney to look us over. Eddy Gandler was almost an annual visitor to our house and we loved having him here. Eddy and his wife Beth Ravit are a wonderful couple, generous to the core. Actually, both of them were married before, and Larry and Ronnie are Eddy's children, while Lauren is Beth's daughter.

Eddy told me that Sadie and Rose, the two sisters of Moishe Halm's wife Golde Goldenberg, had been living in the U.S. Anna, Rose's only surviving daughter, was already in her 90s, and living with her husband Morris in California. Moishe and Golde's two daughters, Sarah (Sure-Rifke) and Blanche (Bleema), as well as their brother Jack (Yechil), had migrated to the USA, surviving the Holocaust. But sadly, the other offspring in Jasina— Rachel, Bince, Beile and Dovid — had perished in the Holocaust.

I learned that Sarah arrived in the USA in 1914, at the tender age of sixteen years. There she apparently met and married Julius Spieler, who was not a well man. He passed away when Sarah was barely 35 years of age. They had three children: Golde, barely 9, Sylvia, 5, and little Dorothy, 3, when Julius died, and Sarah never remarried. True to her Jewish religion, she devoted her life to her three daughters, and they still remember her with great kindness. Their mother was described to me as "Exceptionally kind, generous, proud, stubborn, self-sacrificing and uncomplaining." I do hope that in the great beyond she still continues to keep a watchful eye on her multiplying family and derives pleasure from their many achievements.

---

3   Bleema (Blanche) Halm (1903-1999) was a daughter of Moishe Halm and Golde Goldenberg. Moishe was the son of our original ancestors in Tchorna Tisa Avrom Dovid and Sure-Yente Halm.

Bleema, Moishe and Golde's other surviving daughter was married to Phillip Gandler for 63 years. Bleema and Phillip had two living sons in the New York/New Jersey area, named Murray and Edward (Eddy).

On a visit to Closter, New Jersey, in 1995 I pleaded with Eddy to take me to see his mother, and it was a most rewarding experience. Mother Bleema was already in her nineties, and totally preoccupied with the past, with no appreciation of her surroundings. I was anxious to speak to her in my Jasina mother language, my *mamelushen*, but this made no impression on her. So I just cuddled her, and this made more sense than my *mamelushen*. Realising that Cousin Bleema Gandler was my closest surviving relative, I shed a few tears.

The two boys had made a conscious effort to keep their mother alive for as long as it was humanly possible. This impressed me immensely. Although their mother suffered from senile dementia and didn't even recognise her sons, they visited her two or three times a week and employed a nurse for her, who came in daily to prepare her meals and manage her flat. Murray and Eddy thought that the familiar surroundings would keep their mother alive a bit longer. I would say this was magnificent devotion to a mother: she didn't even know her two sons, but that made no difference to them. For them she had been an exceptional 'Mom'!

My bond with Cousin Bleema stretched over 70 years or more. In fact, she was my oldest blood relative in the world, and reminiscing with her was a real privilege. I remember closing my eyes quite often, when I was with her, and imagining that I was cuddling my beloved great-grandma Bruche. do hope that dear Cousin Bleema has met up with her family on the other side … amen.

I was able to understand the old lady in Closter very well. My elderly mother, who had been living far from me, in Beersheva, had often ignored me when I was in the house; like Cousin Bleema, she had also kept herself alive on her precious memories.

My dear mother had often looked at homes for the aged in Beersheva, but all of them wanted to be given her possessions before she passed on. I still recall how my mother used to kiss the architraves of her house every time she returned home. That little dwelling meant a lot to her. I gather that Cousin Bleema's sons also encountered a similar pre-dicament in New Jersey, and that is why they decided to pay a minder instead.

Had Murray and Eddy placed their mother in a home, she would have perished long before, but in her familiar surroundings, life had a lot of meaning. I recall she talked to people who were no longer with us, but that discourse did sustain her through the years.

Being in Closter with Bleema suddenly rekindled my feelings for my mother. Cousin Bleema seemed like my mother in many respects. So the Closter detour was certainly therapeutic for me, and I was able to shed a few precious tears as well.

When my mother's time came, she was found on the kitchen floor a few days after she died in 1998. I wasn't even there to bury her — she was buried before I arrived back in Israel — and I regret that very much. I went out to the cemetery, and shed my tears there. My mother was 93 years old. It had given her enormous satisfaction to survive the Jewish Holocaust, see the establishment of the State of Israel, and manage a prosperous business in the process.

In 1998, after my dear mother passed away in Israel and I had settled her affairs there, I decided to visit Eddy Gandler's family again. Well, I was suitably impressed. The Gandlers lived in an elegant, one-storey house, on a lavish property, outside the city. Their garden has a num-ber of mature pine trees and plenty of squirrels. While I was there, the Gandlers arranged a family reunion for the Saturday afternoon, and relatives began arriving from far and wide. It was a wonderful op-portunity for me to meet most of my American relations, and I was so grateful to Eddy and Beth for this. It gave me an opportunity to meet my many distant cousins.

The afternoon generated a whole lot of questions, most of which I was unable to answer, but my relations did make a lasting impression on me. They asked me many questions, but I could not tell them why their relatives departed Jasina soon after World War I.

There were so many unfamiliar faces, all claiming to be descendants of my relations; I was humbled. They had arrived to meet a relic from the distant past, and quiz him anxiously about relatives he had never known. It was a lapse of over sixty years, which transferred me fair and square into my childhood. I hardly knew any of their relations and to be fair, they did not know mine, either. So from this aspect, the gathering was purely social.

However, I managed to find out here that Adel Tessler and Dori Eisikovits were blood sisters, though hardly anyone could swear to this. In the old days, Jewish parents often kept their unmarried surnames after the wedding; this was a minhag.[4] Therefore it wasn't unusual for two Jewish siblings to have different last names — one the mother's and one the father's. Tessler and Eisikovits are good examples of this. No one ever questioned this anomaly in Jewish practice. Certainly the orthodox Rabbi, who was only interested in first names, solemnised the weddings without surnames — it was the first names that were all important. To be called to the Torah, I needed only to know my father's Hebrew name—I was 'Moishe, the son of Yosel.'

Yechil, Bleema's brother arrived in the USA safe and sound after the Holocaust. When he noticed that there were no other Yechils around, he changed his name to Jack. This change Americanised him, but managing the spoken language was still a problem. Then Jack became a butcher's apprentice, and things were looking up, but he still continued speaking Yiddish. I gather his boss must have been of the same persuasion. In any case, Jack's trade required no communication with customers, and the slaughtered animals never chatted with him either.

However, being young and eager, Jack soon picked up the language, and began browsing around for a young wife. Soon he met a girl named Bertha, who stole his heart. Now, there were plenty of other girls around, but Jack made up his mind.. The story about Bertha goes like this: she was Hungarian but became ill in Maramoros Sziget, Romania and her life was in danger, so they changed her name to Bat-ya, meaning daughter of G-d. You see, in Romania they believed that the Angel of Death hovered everywhere and Jews were particularly vulnerable, so this name change was a life-saver. And so Bat-ya, recovered, and undertook the journey to the USA, and that is where she met Jack Halm. And Jack, my distant cousin, eventually married Bat-ya

---

4   Hebrew for an accepted tradition or group of traditions in Judaism

Greenberg, and they had two children: Herbert and Harriet. Herbert served and fell in the Korean War, and his sister Harriet trained as a family planner.

Harriet Halm married Dr E. Jack Harris, a successful obstetrician and gynaecologist, who apparently delivered nine thousand babies in a professional lifetime of 35 years. They had three sons, and Harriet still lives in their attractive house at Massapequa, N.Y.

Harriet's father Jack had nurtured childhood ambitions to settle in Palestine, but his military circumstances took him to the USA. When Bat-ya passed away Jack decided to move to the State of Israel. There he lived for another six years, fulfilling his long-held wish. Daughter Harriet travelled to Israel to bury her dear father in the Holy Land.

I dare say that many other Jews from Jasina would have wished to be buried in Israel well. The Good Book prognosticates that when the Meshiach comes, all the dead will rise and assemble at the gates of the Holy Land. My erstwhile cousin Jack will be among them. If I pray hard enough, my dear great-grandmother Bruche, my darling grandmother Bince, my mother Nelly and the most adored Azriel and Blimka Feldman with their three children will all be there.

Chapter 39

My mother's later years

I remember those post-war years when everything was unsettled, and the population movements were enormous. Everybody was going off somewhere.

I know I had no urge to return to Tchorna Tisa after the Holocaust, but other people did — not to recoup their properties, but simply to see if anyone had returned from the Holocaust. Even my mother went back, after a fifteen month incarceration[5], to find that the house had been demolished and the neighbours didn't want to know her. So she packed her bag and went to Czechoslovakia, where, as a Holocaust survivor, she was given a self-contained flat in Usti nad Labem.

She longed to be reunited with her half-siblings and their families after the Holocaust. Now, the pre-war relationship between the siblings had not been the best, but the Holocaust changed many people's perceptions about sibling relationships. When survivors returned to the world of the living they began scouring the Earth for lost relations.

My mother also took the initiative to contact her two half-sisters in the USA, and the correspondence flourished. She also discovered that her two half-brothers had survived the Holocaust in Romania and were contemplating moving to Israel, as she was. Having endured a silence of twenty years or more, she began corresponding with them in Ti-

---

5   My father never mentioned where she was sent, however I assume she was with him in Mateszalka and Auschwitz – Peter Halm

misoara, and received very encouraging replies. I was delighted to hear this. Eventually Yidde and Hersh and their families migrated to Israel, and the separation was ended at last. The sister and the two brothers were reunited.

When my mother went to Israel in 1948 she settled in Gedera, where she became acquainted with Tovie Wald, a little man, even smaller than her. They decided to marry and move to a property in Beersheva. Beersheva was in the desert, and the dunam[6] of land the Government gave them was in the old part of the city. So they moved there and set up home together. Their home was attached to another house, but this was of little consequence, because the land was quite substantial. So Tovie began planting fruit trees and vegetables, and my mother set up a little kiosk selling drinks, confectionery and snacks to the neighbourhood school kids.

Then Tovie got a job building roads, but he wasn't a particularly strong man; he had spent a few years in German extermination camps and now it was catching up with him. But mother's kiosk was doing particularly well, and together they made a reasonable living.

Tovie developed a variety of illnesses, and was forced to give up the road work. He lingered for a while and then died, leaving my mother on her own again. She remained on the property for a good few years; while the kiosk flourished, however, Tovie's garden was neglected. The fruit trees perished in the desert heat, and only some hardy shrubs remained around the house.

After some years, the task of running the kiosk became too much, and mother gradually reduced the stock. Then, as luck would have it, a buyer came and bought the kiosk as a going concern.

So now, for the first time in years, my mother could visit friends and renew her acquaintance with her brothers, Yidde and Hersh. Though all three of them were now living in the same little country, their worlds diverged beyond recognition. Yidde and his family settled near the ocean, in Haifa, while brother Hersh found himself in an old people's home, not far from Beersheva.

---

6   A unit of land area enclosing 1000 square metres.

My mother had a lot of time to catch up, so she made a point of spending as much time as she could with her brother Yidde and wife Tetsa on the Mediterranean coast. I remember her mentioning the wonderful experiences she had walking hand-in-hand with her long lost brother on the sands of independent Israel. She told me that those hours were her most cherished interludes. It seemed that time had swept aside all the family bitterness and a new beginning dawned as my mother acquired two formerly estranged brothers in, of all places, the Holy Land.

Although mother spoke Hebrew fluently, with her brothers she conversed in good old Hungarian. From all accounts, Uncle Yidde was still a remarkable man with a wonderful sense of humour, and my mother enjoyed his effervescence and charming humility. I could just visualise them walking hand-in-hand on the beaches of Tel Aviv or Haifa. Had they ever dreamed that the Jews would someday possess that homeland? Hardly. Now my mother and her favourite brother could saunter on the beach and reminisce about another world somewhere in the Carpathian Mountains, or at the other end of the globe. Oh, how mother enjoyed those glorious summer days with her brother, and one can only lament the wasted decades they spent in annoyed silence.

Uncle Hersh was another of my relatives that I had never met in person until I visited him in an old people's home in Israel. As a socially conscious health worker I had a particular interest in seeing how the elderly were treated in Israel. Consequently, I visited a number of old-aged facilities, for both rich and poor, and was appalled at what I saw. The homes for the aged that were supported by overseas concerns were not that bad, however I found that the conditions were unbelievable in the ones run by the State and private Israeli businesses.

As I understand it, the State finances private concerns to keep the old peoples' homes in operation and they are so lucrative that we see them mushrooming everywhere. However, government supervision is sparse and the homes suffer the same fate as most publicly owned institutions. There is apparently enormous corruption in this area and the incentives are great. Consequently, the old people are desperately neglected.

My Uncle Hersh was a reserved elderly man whose wife had passed away years earlier, and he was now spending his old age in despicable circumstances in a privately owned homes for the elderly. My mother and I visited him there, and I was sickened to the pit of my stomach by the inhuman conditions to which the inmates were subjected. Uncle Hersh's mattress was soaked in excreta and so was the bedding of many of the other inmates. The stench in the wards was overpowering.

This was by far the most debilitating sight I have ever seen and believe me, I have seen plenty. The Jewish hospital in the Ebensee extermination camp, with eight inmates to each bed, was nothing compared to this debacle. I mean, we were in a Jewish State, where the elderly inmates were simply left to die in their own stench,and there was no shortage of other elderly people to take their place. Even the Nazi extermination camps would not have tolerated this state of affairs. There, the wards were inspected daily and the beds had to be spic and span, or heads would roll.

Uncle Hersh did have a married son, David, in Beersheva, and a daughter, Chaya, in Jerusalem, but they hardly ever visited the old man. Had they visited him and taken an interest in his wellbeing, I'm sure they would not have tolerated these conditions.

Of course, not all the institutions for the elderly looked like the one. The elderly who were able to pay had immaculate places, but the ones who couldn't, the Israeli poor, were left to rot. Most of them were people who had fought in all the wars and survived. And what about the poor Kibbutz members who toiled on the land all their lives? And the Holocaust survivors who arrived penniless? Who looks after the poor and the incapacitated in the Jewish State? Have the Israeli Government and the social system discarded them altogether? Are they to be left to the heartless scalpers who run these despicable old people's homes? I mean, how can the democratic State of Israel reconcile these discrepancies in the treatment of its elder citizenry?

Seeing the conditions in the facility where Uncle Hersh lived, I certainly could not condemn my mother to that sort of life. I am sure that my mother observed the neglect of her brother and made up her mind never to enter one of those institutions. I remember that she kissed the architraves of the front door when she returned to Beersheva; little wonder that she was so determined to die in her own house, which she finally did four years later.

Chapter 40

A visit to my homeland

When I left Prague for Australia, the situation in Czechoslovakia was already in a state of flux and Communism was very much on the horizon. Well, for the next 30 odd years the Communists reigned supreme, until the breaking of the Iron Curtain.

In 1992 Ruth and I decided to visit my Eastern European past. We decided to go to Prague on our return journey and book our first flight into Budapest. From there we intended to go to Uzhorod, and eventually Jasina.

As Hungary played such an important part in the occupation of Karpatolya, I can't very well leave its activities out of the picture. Hungary occupied Podkarpatska Russ for over five years, and it is fitting and proper that I devote more than a passing glance at its machinations in Karpatolya.

In 1941, one in every 16 Hungarians was Jewish.[7] However, after the Holocaust the numbers were reduced, and you could barely find one Jew among a hundred citizens.

The historical perspective is that the Hungarians descended from the Finish and Turkish tribes and settled in the Plains of Anyaorszag a

---

7   The census of January 1941 found that 6.2% of the population, i.e., 846,000 people, were considered Jewish according to the racial laws of that time. Wikipedia

good few centuries ago. There they nurtured their traditions and customs while eating goulash and chicken paprika.

Over the centuries, Hungary underwent many upheavals: the Tartars, the Ottomans, the Austrian Rule, the demand for independence in the 1800s and the formation of the Austro-Hungarian Empire in 1867. During the era of this last predicament, Franz-Josef I of Austria was also crowned King of Hungary. Then in World War I Hungary lost its independence, and the Soviets helped to establish a Russian style dictatorship. Subsequently, Admiral Miklos von Nagybanya Horthy assumed power and turned Hungary into a monarchy — without a Monarch. Horthy bacsi[8] declared himself Regent, and remained in power until 1957.

He was there when the Hungarian Jews were deported to Auschwitz, and he maintained his staunch support for Adolf Hitler and the Third Reich. In return, Hitler promised Horthy all the captured provinces, and as a result of this Horthy signed a military pact with Nazi Germany and Italy.

Hitler occupied Czechoslovakia and promptly gave Karpatolya and Southern Slovakia to the Hungarians. He also gave them half of Transylvania, and this boosted the Hungarian population by some 4,108,000. In return, Hungary joined the Axis in the invasion of Russia, but it's forces incurred severe losses. So now Hungary asked for a separate armistice, but instead Germany invaded its former ally, and Horthy Miklos was imprisoned and remained in prison until the Russian forces liberated Hungary in 1945.

But although the Russians liberated the Hungarian Republic, the country didn't get its independence until November 1945, some six months after the fall of Nazi Germany. I still remember the deeds of Hungarian criminals in the forests of Tchorna Tisa, where they hunted and killed the poor escaping Jews from Poland. I can neither forgive nor forget these criminal activities. Hungary was certainly a willing partner in the extermination of the Jewish people.

In 1992, I was in two minds as to whether to set foot on Hungarian soil, but after much trepidation we set off. We had arranged to stay

---

with a lady called Edit in central Budapest, so when our plane from Rome landed we took a taxi to Edit's address. She was expecting our arrival, and had prepared the room for us. She was a very practical, down-to-earth individual.

Ruth had developed a serious chest infection during our flight from Sydney to Rome, so we asked Edit to call a doctor. Curiously the young medico arrived in a chauffeur-driven limousine and Edit explained that in Hungary all female doctors had male drivers. The doctor gave Ruth a thorough examination and duly prescribed an antibiotic. Since neither Ruth nor I were Hungarian citizens, the doctor thought it would be simpler to make the prescription in Edit's name, and so this was done. The medical and pharmacological services were free in Hungary, but foreigners had to pay. We were foreigners, but the good doctor had the presence of mind to cheat the Hungarian medical system. Then Edit whispered to me in her best German: "Offer the doctor a substantial gratuity."

After this episode, I went out and got us a hot, delicious goulash soup, which we enjoyed immensely, and we retired for the night. We were staying in a historic, multi-storey building in Budapest, which had an old-world charm about it. Edit's flat was on the first floor. The concrete stairs were wide and well-worn, and an enormous gate opened up to a set of stables, hidden in the backyard. It was obvious that the building and the stables had belonged to a prosperous Hungarian nobleman, long gone to his eternal rest. The property was now somewhat dilapidated, but it still had grandiose high ceilings; these were excellent for summer ventilation, but hardly accommodating in the freezing winters.

We still had no visas for Zakarpatska Ukraina, and I didn't even know how to get them. So we went to the railway station, and discovered there a daily train going to the Ukrainian border. Although I spoke many languages, Hungarian was not one of them. So we had some difficulty making these travel arrangements.

We found the Hungarian bureaucracy exceedingly lethargic. Now, I know that we didn't speak the language and didn't ask the right questions, but their answers were grossly disjointed. So we quickly came to the conclusion that bloody foreigners were not welcome in Hungary. I wondered how this God-forsaken country would fare in a united

Europe. I got the impression that they also hated the Communist bureaucracy — but why were they at ease with its impregnable lethargy? We found this exceeding laziness all over Budapest. We did make a genuine effort to ask questions, in broken Hungarian, but many times we were ignored — so we foreigners concluded that the system was at fault.

I visited the IBUSZ Travel Agency which supposedly handled trips to all parts of the globe, so I told them that we wanted to go to Zakarpatska Ukraina, and was then left alone without further help. During the Hungarian occupation of Karpatolya, I had learned a great many marching tunes, but all of them were full of anti-Semitic references and not at all fitting in the Hungarian travel agencies. So I soon came to the conclusion that the Hungarians ignored anything they didn't want to understand.

Then I discovered another travel agency, called MA'V Tours, in Nandor Street, but they sent us back to IBUSZ. I was disgusted with this treatment and the Hungarian bureaucracy, but after this someone suggested that we go to the Central Railway Station. Well, it was lunchtime, and I was in no mood to trudge around town, so I went home.

Meanwhile, Ruth was still medicating herself and poor Edit had a severe bout of vertigo, but she did contact the Soviet Embassy, and was told to ring on a working day. So by this time we had lost all hope of getting out of Hungary, and decided to nourish ourselves instead. The soup I brought home was cold and unappetising, but I had discovered in the process that all Hungarian business was conducted in the mornings. So the next day I set out nice and early, securing a railway booking from Budapest to near the Carpathian border, without any fuss.

It was fortuitous that we were not on a tight travelling schedule, or these delays would certainly have caused havoc with our itinerary. But our landlady, who recovered from her vertigo, was an absolute tower of strength — ever helpful and co-operative in matters administrative. Edit did some calling and found out that Zakarpatska Ukraina had no Consulate in Budapest, and that entry visas to Karpatolya were obtainable at the border. She also found that a train left Budapest every morning for Zahony and then crossed the border to Csop, in Zakarpatska Ukraina. This also deserved a special 'hallelujah!'

In Sydney, I spent 35 years in diagnostic radiography and attended a great many international conferences during that time. Visiting foreign cities, I developed the habit of seeking out and participating in many synagogue services.

We discovered that the city was full of Jews, of all varieties. Budapest even had a Yeshiva, for higher Jewish learning — something that we thought the Holocaust had done away with forever. So in Budapest I sought out this Jewish life, and this took me to a small house of worship not far from the Great Synagogue. It appeared that the Great had sustained a lot of damage over the years and was being renovated, so the *Shabbes* services were held in this smaller *Shule*. It was raining in Budapest and I was soaked to the skin, but I would not have missed this service. The orthodox service was pretty similar to ours in Maroubra, except for the Hungarian prayer books.

Then before I knew it, the service was over, and I felt rejuvenated. Usually I find when visiting a foreign community I was invited to congregants' homes for lunch. Ah, in Budapest, there were plenty of 'Shabbat Shalom's, but not one invitation for *Kiddush*. What is it with these Hungarian Jews, I wondered; they called me up to the Torah, but are they too stingy to offer me a glass of wine?

By Sunday, Ruth was feeling a bit better, and so we went down to the Central Railway Station and bought our tickets to Csop. Then, we sauntered down to the elegant Vaci Utca to look at the window displays, and splashed out on two white coffees. Who would go all the way to Budapest and deny himself the luxury of an expensive coffee while watching the world go by? Then we planned to walk along the Danube and cross the beautiful Elizabeth Bridge, but the inclement weather put an end to that, so we returned home. In the late afternoon we ventured out again and took a bus ride across the Danube and into the Budapest Hills. It was an interesting journey, but we were leaving next day for Zakarpatska Ukraina and had to return home to pack.

Our train left Budapest at 6.05am and by nine o'clock it passed through Debreczen. On the train Ruth befriended two women, Ludmila and her daughter Veronika. and now we had good company. They were returning to Mukachevo, in Ukraine from Budapest, where they often travelled to stock up on things that were in short supply. Ruthie managed her sign language rather well, and the two Russians practised their cultivated expressions, conveying plenty of good mirth. Only very occasionally was my assistance required — when the three of them were stumped. Then Ludmila offered us accommodation for the night at her house in Mukachevo. We gladly accepted.

We learned from them that almost everybody in Zakarpatska Ukraina travelled to Budapest and lugged things back to the Ukraine. But, we asked, with all this trade going on, how come there was such a shortage of things in Zakarpatska Ukraina? Mother and daughter explained that people dealt, among other things, in perishable goods, which needed constant replenishment. In any case, the Hungarian authorities appeared to lose hardly any sleep over this trade, and did nothing to impede it. Did any of the Ukrainians deal in contraband? I asked, but this was laughed off. The trade was obviously illegal, but who was going to impose any fines when the Hungarian industries were flourishing? The railway authorities were also making huge profits from this business, and beyond that nobody cared.

Long before the train reached to the Ukrainian border, the Ukrainian guards came to inspect our passports and walked away with them. For eight long hours they were confiscated and we were stateless. When they passed by us again, Ludmila made her Russian outrage known, but the Ukrainian thugs simply ignored her; the passports were eventually returned to us.

My accrued hostilities against the Hungarians were many, but one thing had to be acknowledged —their trains ran on time. Now, arriving at the frontier, the Ukrainian border guards demanded entry visas, and since Ruth and I had none, they shunted us off to a separate queue where the officialdom dealt only in American dollars. Well, fortunately I still had some US currency, so the two visas set us back a cool 100 dollars, or 32,000 Ukrainian Coupons, the temporary currency issued at the time, as Soviet currency had become worthless. Then I told Ludmila about this, and she promptly flew into a rage, but it was a wasted effort. We knew that one never haggled with the border guards. They were simply doing their duty — but, I asked, did they have to be so threatening about it? Well, it was either the fortune in dollars, or jail, so we quickly settled for the dollars.

After we arrived at Csop, I left Ruth with the women while they got their luggage together on the platform, and went to look around — and was unable to get back to them. The Ukrainian throng was now moving out to the exit, and they were determined not to let anyone back in; it was a fight against the tide. Then, to make matters worse, the station was in total darkness and trains were whizzing past in all directions. This station seemed to be a cross-road for all trains heading East, and as far as I could tell they were all headed to Moscow.

After much difficulty we reunited and struggled onto the train for Mukachevo. Ruth and I realised that we had no tickets for this train, so we left our luggage and returned to the station to join the throng. Well, this took an inordinate amount of time, and eventually we had our tickets, but were quite resigned to missing the train; however, once outside, we realised that the train was still waiting for us. Now it was 1.30am, and we were weary and despondent.

It was around 4.00am when we arrived in Mukachevo and it was absolute bedlam again. Ludmila left to secure a taxi while we did the luggage unloading, and the Ukrainian throng seemed to pursue Ludmila into the streets. Actually, this was the most lucrative time for the taxi drivers, and even people with private cars made a killing. But some old Babushkas never even bothered with the taxis, carrying their fortunes on their heads instead.

Thinking back about all the unmitigated risks we took, the hair-raising separations and the uncomfortable train rides, I wondered if all travel in Zakarpatska Ukraina was as arduous as ours. Perhaps it wasn't, and this was only something that Ruth and I experienced.

Ludmila returned with a cab in tow, and we loaded it up to the rafters. The experienced cab driver looked at the load and began haggling over the price. He soon increased the fare, but we didn't quibble over it. The driver insisted on payment in advance, and Ludmila obliged. Although Ludmila's house was only a short distance away from the station, the pile of luggage was quite enormous, and we could not have carried it there ourselves. Inside the taxi there was just enough room to accommodate Ludmila and the driver, while Ruth, Veronica and I walked the short distance to the house.

The taxi driver delivered his load, and when we got to the house the luggage was on the footpath, and the cab was nowhere to be seen. I found it rather interesting that neither the Ukrainians nor the Hungarians bothered about the influx of goods, and we concluded once more that the Hungarian economy was doing particularly well out of this chaotic affair.

Then Ludmila unlocked the door. We managed to get into the house with our luggage, and just flopped down exhausted.

The house Ludmila and Veronica lived in was set back from the street, and had an old-world charm about it. However, the atmosphere inside was something else. Most of the galvanised water pipes were rusted through, so the water closet was also on the blink, and relied heavily on buckets of water being poured down the toilet. Consequently, there was always a resilient stench in the house, which took some tolerating.

In the late afternoon Ludmila began cooking dinner. Ruth and I also contributed to the evening meal, and it was enjoyed immensely. We added our Hungarian cheese to the macaroni, and this proved to be a satisfying meal.

I was worried about our heavy cases. We wouldn't be able to lug them all the way to Jasina. But Ludmila solved that problem by suggesting that we leave the cases at her place. We needed hardly any persuasion.

Then the girls moved some furniture around, Ludmila began improvising our bedding for the night, and soon Ruth and I were safely tucked in bed. We had a good night's sleep, and in the morning began organising our trip to Jasina . Ruthie and I decided to share our Hungarian provisions with the girls, and Ludmila added some fried chips to the scrambled eggs, which made a jolly good breakfast.

It was Tuesday, 8 September 1992. After breakfast the two women took us to the railway station to buy tickets, with our bags loaded on the back of Veronica's bicycle. We took only things that were absolutely essential for the trip. Soon we found a bus leaving for Jasina. Each bus ticket cost 300 Ukrainian Coupons, and this payment also enabled us to reserve our seats.

We still had an hour's wait, so we decided to do a brief sightseeing tour of Mukachevo. We went for a walk, with the loaded bicycle in tow.

Well, I soon realised that Ludmila's old street, with its ancient trees, was certainly the most beautiful of all in the city. The buildings around the station were old and very neglected. Mukachevo was the second largest city in Podkarpatska Russ, and it used to be the jewel in Czechoslovakia's crown. I well remember some of the proud Jews who had sons in the Munkacs Yeshiva[9]. That was the city that housed some of the most important Yeshivot in the world.

Now its past glories are but a distant memory, and the few Jews who live there are seldom seen in the hostile streets. Mukachevo will never again achieve the lofty heights it cherished before World War II; it is now a neglected city with a Jewish past. I don't quite know which part of Mukachevo we covered, but the little we saw of it brought feelings of sadness, and tears to my eyes.

We made our way back to the bus station, and farewelled our friends. I was already anxious to get some privacy and shed a few precious tears for the world we had lost.

We boarded the bus; all was well until the populace came aboard with their parcels and animals. I soon realised that this was not going to be a pleasant journey. Another wave to Ludmila and Veronica, and then the bus turned around and we were on our way. It was a long way to Jasina, the place where had I spent the best part of my first 20 years.

The journey had barely started when my thoughts were with my lost little schoolmates. As I reminisced, tears channelled down my face, more for the lost children than anything else. Oh, the memories were overpowering my soul. How will I react, I thought, when I see our

---

9   Munkacs (Hungarian; Mukachevo, Ukr.; Mukacevo, Czech and Slov.) was the commercial capital of the Transcarpathian region of Ukraine. Its many names reflect the cultural crossroads of its location. The town belonged to Hungary until 1920, to Czechoslovakia (1920-1938), and again to Hungary from 1938-1945. The Jewish population of Munkacs grew from 2,131 in 1825 to 5,049 in 1891 (almost 50 percent of the total population) to 7,675 in 1910 (about 44 percent). By 1921, the 10,000 Jews still made up about half the residents, though by 1930, the proportion had dropped to 43 percent, with a little over 11,000 Jews. The Jews of Munkacs constituted 11 percent of the Jewry of Subcarpathian Rus.

house and property being farmed by other people? What will I feel when I walk the streets I once frequented every day? Oh, my lovely Tchorna Tisa, has it changed at all? Will the snow-covered Hoverla mountain still provide the backdrop to the town? And the pine forests, will they still be there? I also tried, vainly, to put the little faces of my schoolmates in order, but the tears quickly flooded my face again. The Jewish Holocaust has put an end to all we have cherished in this world.

Now, almost 50 years later, since that fateful *Pesach* day in 1944, I was returning to Tchorna Tisa. My mind slowly drifted to all the other Jews I used to know there; alas, they never returned. Names came to mind and faces reappeared, but they vanished just as quickly. I was glad Ruthie was with me, and appreciated her enormous understanding.

This visit had to be made. I had nurtured this attachment for almost 50 years, and even the Jewish Holocaust was not able to diminish the intensity of it. I thought of my dear great-grandma Bruche, my loving Boobe Bince, the Feldman family, and our whole neighbourhood; oh, they were all so dear to me.

Then I realised that this was a pleasure trip, and all the depressing thoughts had to be put aside. We might never pass this way again. The weather was beautiful, and visibility was excellent. The main road out of Mukachevo quite good, and the autumn fields were abundant. As the journey progressed, more and more people boarded the bus. We travelled on that bus through Zakarpatska Ukraina all the way to Jasina. But would you believe it — for some inexplicable reason our long-suffering bus never exceeded 30 km per hour.

We noticed it everywhere; unadulterated poverty. We passed through a great many towns and villages, and all of them had plenty of empty shops, inundated with flies and peeling walls. They had no goods on display, but the windows were extravagantly colourful. Oh, don't get me wrong — they were decorative, but vacant. Were they hoping for better times? Was this a matter of hopeful anticipation, or wistful neglect? More like the latter, I assumed.

Then, in the late afternoon, we edged closer to the mountains, and there was a distinct nip in the air. Was this from the lateness of the hour, or the influence of the mountains? Hard to say; probably the latter. Then the bus passed through Rachov, and we knew there was a distance of just 30 kilometres to go. The number of standing passengers had thinned out, but the bus was still in no great hurry.

The anticipation of seeing my dear old Jasina was killing me; I had been away from it for almost 50 years. Now in my mind I was already picturing the Czech school, the Iron Bridge, the fruit markets, the Cheder, Yance's abode, and my cousin Yoshka's tailoring shop. Which of them would still be there after all this time?

Chapter 41

Jasina at last

The bus crossed another wooden bridge, and came to a sudden halt. We climbed out, and found ourselves on the outskirts of town. It was all very strange, and I didn't recognise it at all.

It was now seven o'clock in the evening, and there were still a few hours of sunshine left, but I was totally disorientated. "Which way from here?" I asked Ruth, but before I could say any more she said, "Let's follow the crowd". We set out on our way, and I wondered if my Czech school would still be there and if I would recognise it. I was rather anxious to see my primary school building, but I knew it was still some distance away. But Ruth was now more interested in the town, so we accelerated our pace.

We had been given a recommendation of a place to stay in Jasina, at the home of a woman named Natasha. On the side of the road I approached two local women with my piece of paper in hand. They looked at the address and volunteered to take us there. Well, along the way we chatted, and to my amazement, one of them was a schoolmate of mine, from all those many years ago. This quickly melted the ice, and we began recalling names of former classmates. Then my old schoolmate invited us to have a look at her school album, but the meeting with our landlady, Natasha, made this impossible. You see, the two visitors took us right up to Natasha's door, and when the door was opened, and my schoolmate saw who lived there, an unpleasant exchange of words took place, and our guides left in an agitated hurry.

So within a few short minutes I had discovered a schoolmate and then promptly lost her forever; rather lamentable, but life is like that. I concluded that the women's arguments were not ours, nor did we have to endure them on this short trip. But these unexpected hostilities also negated my chances of ever seeing that school album.

We had arrived safely in the town I longed to see, but our landlady Natasha's priorities were not ours. She immediately filled tumblers of Horiuka, and we drank cheerfully. Then she showed us to our room; we rested up a while, and we went out.

When we had arrived in Jasina I had noticed a half-finished, multi-storey building. I was told that the Russians had started it, but never completed it. It hadn't been there before. This one high-rise in Jasina attested to a recent Russian presence; these were holiday flats, for the Communist apparatchiks, but still only half-finished. I also noted that the Town Hall, the solitary bank, the indispensable post office, and some tourist hostels now enjoy higher levels of visual luxury.

I discovered that my primary school had been demolished. It used to sit on an elevated piece of land, diagonally across from the pharmacy, but it was no longer there.

I hardly recognised old Jasina. The town now had an enormously wide road, with unattractive flower beds in the middle, stretching along the dilapidated shopping mall. I remembered how all the Jewish shops had been clustered together in the old days, but this had all changed. I suspected that many of the demolished rows of houses might have been Jewish homes. They were sacrificed for the wider road, which served no useful purpose.

The old shopping centre, with the cakes, the tobacconists, the iron-mongers, and the tailors, as well as the prosperous businesses — Gallitz and Rosenthal's school requisites, and Pashkess — had vanished. There were very few shops, and all were neglected. The food shops had no produce in them, though the hardware stores were well stocked. The elderly people we met hastened to assure us that in the good old days, the shops had all been full; now all the streets were lit up, yet the shops were empty.

Nightfall brought little flickering globes to life, and with them, an overpowering silence. The centre of Jasina now had high cement pylons, with small electric bulbs. The high pylons gave off more light to the sky than they did to the people on the ground. Those pylons were all fabricated in the Soviet Union and gave towns a uniform look.

We saw no new streets, and the ones I knew were in bad disrepair. Another night-time innovation we observed was queuing: the populace stood in line for their food rations— bread and other necessities of life. At six in the afternoon, the queues would form outside the single bakery as the whole town lined up for the bread rations.

The old people we used to know had passed on, and their descendants knew hardly any Jews. Jasina now had a mixture of Russians and Ukrainians. Our old Rabbinical scholars had perished in the Holocaust. So Jasina had no synagogues and no Jews; only the Jewish cemetery up on the hill bore witness to the period when being Jewish was actually rewarding.

The old bridge had decorative spans and style; it was the pride and joy of the town. It looked like a shorter version of the Sydney Harbour Bridge, majestically arching across the Lazeshtina River. The newer Soviet replacement was ugly. It had none of the structural elegance of the old bridge, and the majestic arches had been removed altogether — the coat-hangers had vanished. The humiliation was too much to bear. Did the old bridge really need replacing? Could a coat of paint have saved the bridge? Who knows.

I can still remember the importance of "Di Azene Brick" (its name in Yiddish), because anything that happened in town invariably took place on one or the other side of this bridge. My Czech school was on the far side of the bridge, and Tzivie's fruit mart languished right next to it, on the other side. Similarly, cousin Yoshka's tailor shop and my old Cheder were almost in a parallel line, but in different directions.

There were more people in Jasina now, and many more houses on the outskirts, but the townsfolk seemed miserable, and fearful of strangers. Even their former colourful garb had now disappeared, and the only sport in town was the nightly gathering in the market place. There, people chatted and joked, and then returned home for the night. We didn't see any pubs or restaurants, apart from the decorative koleba up on the hill. Jasina had been a prosperous town, but I would say that it now had more signs of deprivation. It seemed that the locals' enthusiasm for life had left them. There seemed to be considerable poverty and neglect, presumably since the Ukrainians had secured independence.

I noticed that the popular cinema complex —the Koruna — was gone and so was the ten pin bowling alley, which used to augment my meagre finances.

All this had happened such a long time ago; as we sauntered around in Jasina, I kept explaining to Ruth where all the important places were. The two orthodox synagogues used to face each other defiantly, but now they had gone. The one on the left had been an ancient building; behind it were my *Cheder* and the *Mikvah*, where the Jewish women dipped their ritual sins away. Then, on the other side of the street had stood the new synagogue.

The town's Head Office, the prison cells and the tobacconist were still there, and the empty area where the weekly markets used to be held now had pine trees growing. Before this forest was there, the area used to be empty, and the people brought their animals to sell. But that was 40 or 50 years ago, and in the 1990s one could well ask: "Who needs a forest in the centre of the town?"

Alas, the memories of the past were still firmly riveted in my mind, and no amount of shabby modernity could bring back the Jasina I once loved. Post-war Jasina had its problems. I heard that even the mighty waterways were now choked with sludge, and the flow was barely 20 per cent of what it had once been.

The proud Hutsuls had lost their uniqueness; there was nothing much to admire now. They used to be rugged individuals, but that had all vanished. Though they now had independence, there was no work, and the poverty was palpable. There was no hotel accommodation. We found that the new Ukrainians didn't even talk of the old days; they belonged to a new generation which was more anti-Semitic than the old, and they knew little of the old times. This generation recalled the Russian might with mixed feelings and didn't even remember the Czechs. In the Soviet Union, they had at least had security of employment, price control and goods they enjoyed. Now they had Ukrainian independence, and very little else. The good times had vanished, and when the new Ukrainians talked about them, you were left pondering.

Isn't it strange that in my old age I look back wistfully at the times I once abhorred? The Czechoslovak Republic under its founder, Tomas Garrigue Masaryk, was a fabulous democracy, even in outlying Tchorna Tisa. In those days, all the minorities had security, guaranteed by the nation's constitution. Even the observant Jew in an isolated hamlet in the Carpathian Mountains felt secure; orthodoxy was guaranteed by the State. The people of Jasina were reasonably tolerant, but their daughters seldom made love to Jews. In other words, life was already segregated, but still reasonably harmonious.

All the empty allotments in old Jasina are now thoroughly peopled, and few even remember the Jews. I discovered that it was far healthier to remain silent in Jasina now. Nobody seemed to ask any questions. It was as if the people were afraid to open their mouths.

Many of the residents were Russian, and know nothing of the Jewish tragedy, or they were Ukrainians, who know everything about it and eagerly celebrated our demise. When I asked some Ukrainians if any Jews lived there, they looked at me in utter disbelief. Most of the Ukrainians don't even know what a Jew is, but that has not diminished their hatred. One doesn't have to know a person to revile him. The Ukrainian regime was instilled with a Nazi anti-Semitism to last the Ukrainians an eternity. and I could just imagine the reception any Jew would receive if he tried to reclaim his properties, which are owned by Ukrainians.

We told Natasha that we intended going to Tchorna Tisa, and she immediately expressed a keen interest in coming with us on the Sunday. Not only that, she also wanted to bring all her relatives along and make it a joyous occasion.

Now this did not suit us at all, and we decided to make the trip the following day. I did not want to have a whole procession of people traipsing along on what was supposed to be a sad and solemn occasion. I intended to shed tears and share the Holocaust past with my wife, not strangers. So we walked the six kilometre distance, that I used to walk as a child, and took in all the changes that had occurred in the past 50 years.

Chapter 42

The road to Tchorna Tisa

S o on the Wednesday we set out. The walk to Tchorna Tisa tested my memory, and I tried hard to assemble an image of how it was long ago. Well the month of September is harvest time in Tchorna Tisa, but in 1992, the fields were barely dotted with farm workers. Ah, September used to be the happiest time of the year. Neighbours came to help each other out in the fields and there was singing everywhere. At harvest time, people simply ignored their aching backs.

As Ruthie and I walked, we noted that all the empty land along both sides of the Tchorna Tisa road had been built upon. This means that the population had increased beyond all belief, but how did they all make a living? Well, certainly not in the adjacent forests. The language they spoke was Russian, and we hardly heard a Ruthenian word uttered — a Ukrainian country with a Russian accent?

We walked the very route I had walked every day of the week, and I recalled carrying that heavy rucksack on my back and two weighty milk cans in my hands as a small eight or nine year old, traversing the deep snow.

I remembered the slippery roads, the anti-Semitic onslaughts, the milk spillages and the beatings I got at the end of the day. I also recalled the many times I asked dear Feige, our next door neighbour, to accompany me home because I feared the repercussions — the milk was spilled, and spilled milk never earned any money. That was my childhood in Tchorna Tisa.

As we walked along the same neglected road I had used every school day, I was surprised that the vehicular traffic was so light—the streets were mostly deserted. We only encountered one horse drawn vehicle, with rubber wheels. Rubber wheels what a revelation. In my time, all the heavy wheels and spikes were made of wood and enclosed in metal rims; we could hear the noisy *droshkes* a mile away. Now, the rubber wheels creep up on you and the horse is breathing down your neck, before you realise that you must give way. These rubber wheels are a proper nuisance, but they need no greasing and this means the whole affair is a lot cheaper. In fact, we hardly saw any four legged animals either along the way, or even two legged pedestrians.

I recalled the heavy pine logs that used to be carted to the sawmills and the *darabes* that floated along the Tisa, the Douzhena and the Lazesti-na twice a week. After the trees were felled, the foresters of my day removed the timber debris before new trees were planted. This renewal process gave our Ruthenians their steady employment. However, on this visit in 1992, I was more than shocked. The timber industry was now dead. There was a bare hill in the middle of a dense forest; I was told that the Russians had done this. They had apparently removed the timber and not replanted new trees. I was deeply saddened by this wanton destruction. I realised that the whole forestry industry was dead now.

I pointed out to Ruthie Jan Hamuth's old house, where I had spent many hours. Jan Hamuth was a good schoolmate of mine, and his mother was a contemporary of my mother's. It was a friendship I had always cherished.

Then from there we proceeded up the hill, but none of the dwellings looked familiar any more. Jews were nowhere to be seen. Their prop-erties had been misappropriated by Russians or Ukrainian nationalists; that was another unspoken secret here. The terrain had not changed all that much, and the mountains were still the same, but the population was different.

Some three kilometres from Jasina, we came to the place where Steinkohl's house once stood, but it was no longer there. Then, across the street, the Rosenthals' abode was also missing, and their enormous land holding was now subdivided, with a house on each plot. It once was an infinitely larger property, always waterlogged, and it belonged to the Rosenthal family. This was an enormous holding, and on most of it grew a type of weed that cows never ate. Consequently, the hay from it had to be sold to people who owned horses. Now I don't remember Mrs Rosenthal, but I do recall the three beautiful daughters, and their father's awful habit of hiding outside and waiting for passers-by to solicit a cigarette from. His daughters were very attractive, and I always lamented that I wasn't bigger, or a few years older. Had I been able to add a few years to my age, I would have exploited all the possibilities.

Then there was the old, haunted iron bridge, which I had always feared, but it was also gone. From there we proceeded up the road and came face to face with the little cloister, where the people used to light candles for their dear departed. There used to be an enormous, empty house occupied by ghosts; now that house was also gone, but the little cloister remained. Oh, how fearful I used to be of those flickering lights, with the mythical images they made on the snow. I had many sleepless nights over those flickering candles.

On the same level as the cloister was the fashionable house of the two brothers who had built our abode, but that was no longer there either. Then, on the down-hill run, we didn't recognise any of the houses; we soon reached the Behensky bridge, where our relatives had lived. There was Urtze and his wife Rachel and her children, and the Katz family, in whose house we used to pray on *Shabbes*.

From there we proceeded further, but Beila's attractive house was no longer there. However, Dvoire's old dwelling near the wooden bridge was still standing. We then crossed the bridge and turned right to the public land, where our cows Olga and Lisa grazed and clambered up to the marshes. Those marshes used to be waterlogged and still were on our visit, but much of the land had been salvaged and was being farmed quite successfully.

From there we went on, passing Klocsurek's house on the corner, which was still occupied. In my time, there were thirteen children in that house, and I wondered who was still there now. Then we reached the Bozhenyuk house with the three daughters.

Now across the Tchorna Tisa river, just opposite the old Ruthenian school, they had erected a swinging bridge; I wondered how many brave kids ventured across it when the river was in full flood? However, our Tisa was now peaceful, and the single-file bridge had to be admired.

On the way, we noticed the glistening steeple of the Orthodox Church on the hill; it had a new roof, but they had forgotten to paint it. That church had stood there since my great-great-grandfather's time, and even Godless Communism could not divert the Ukrainian allegiance to God.

The differences were enormous and rather painful to me. The only indisputable evidence of a former Jewish existence was the ancient Jewish cemetery above the town. There was a new barbed wire fence around the cemetery, which certainly prevented the cows from trampling over the old Jewish graves. But the passing of so many decades had certainly taken its toll. A great many of the head-stones had keeled over, or were leaning precariously in mid-air. And even the standing *Matzeives*, or headstones, had inscriptions and dates I could not interpret. The engravings were in a language I could hardly understand.

We were anxious to see the graves of great-grandma Bruche and grandma Bince. We walked up and down the cemetery to try to identify them; we were unable to find my family's graves. Sadly, they must have been overgrown, and the stones levelled.

As we were leaving the cemetery, we noticed three fresh graves. They were fenced off, and had Cyrillic inscriptions on the headstones. Many years previously I had been fairly fluent in the Ruthenian language and could have deciphered inscriptions, but now I was very rusty. The stones were of a recent vintage — 1970, 1971 and 1983. But the last headstone intrigued me, because it bore the Jewish name of Bohorodcsaner. So where had this person come from? One feasible explanation was that this person named Bohorodcsaner had stayed in the Soviet Union after the war and might have expressed a wish to be returned to Jasina . Sounds convincing? Who knows — there were many Bohorodcsaners in Lazeshtina, and this one might well have preferred to be buried in Tchorna Tisa!

Some years later, while travelling in Miami, Florida, I decided to investigate this Bohorodcsaner from Jasina . In my search for the name, I soon discovered a listing for a Bernard Bohorodcsaner, whom I knew from Tchorna Tisa. So I telephoned him, and he told me he was the Bernard Bohorodcsaner whose parents, Risse and Hersh Bohorodcsaner, had had a grocery store in Tchorna Tisa. Soon we were best friends.

When I was a child in Tchorna Tisa, across from Bohorodcsaner's shop lived a friend of mine; he and his goat often came with us to the forest. He had some kind of impediment and used to drift into oblivion, and we often had to remind him about the conversation we were pursuing. I liked this boy, but heaven knows what happened to him after we were taken to Auschwitz.

I invited Bernard Bohorodcsaner to our Miami hotel, and we spent the rest of the afternoon in an excited discussion. I showed him a photo of the Bohorodcsaner grave in Tchorna Tisa, but he didn't know this person. Well, there were a lot of Bohorodcsaners in Lazeshtina, and this one was probably one of them.

I couldn't take my eyes off Bernard Bohorodcsaner. He was my mother's vintage, but still very agile and handsome. We exchanged a whole lot of pleasantries, and reminisced about old times. He told me about his younger brother, Mendel, who perished in the Holocaust; but his sister Judith had survived the camps. "So where is she?" I asked, but he couldn't tell me. A few weeks after meeting Bernard, I heard that he had passed away.

My mind was in turmoil as we left the cemetery. I recalled Boobe Bruche and Boobe Bince with tearful affection. I also remembered Blima, Azriel and their three adoring children — Yitte, Srulek and Avromele; my tears were now flowing freely, and Ruth tried to calm me down.

Later, after I returned to Beersheva, I told my mother all about our experiences in Jasina , as well as the Jewish cemetery. Then she told me that Avrom-Wolf's children bought a headstone for their father and delivered it to his grave. If I had known that, I would have searched for the grave, but we did pace the holy ground many times over, and never noticed my grandfather's name on a headstone. Time has dealt a bitter blow to the graves and many of them are no longer identifiable. It seems as if the earth just swallowed them up.

Ruth and I were both very sad, and shed a few tears for all the years of neglect and forgetfulness. I hope that my dear Boobe Bruche and my darling Boobe Bince noticed our distress and shared our grief ... Amen.

Eventually we neared number 653, where I noticed that our house and stables were no longer there. After much hesitation I decided to knock on the door of the new house and make myself known. Soon a Russian woman appeared, and asked me what I wanted, so in my halting Russian I explained that we used to own this property. I told her that before 1944 we had a nice house there, and our land used to extend from the street right up to the top of that hill. A surprise awaited me.

After listening patiently she then had the gall to tell me to climb the hill and tell the other people to get off her land. Well, I stood there in total disbelief. She said that her family had paid a lot of money and only received half of the land! There was no sorrow in her voice; she simply instructed me to get the other half of the property for her. Apparently, the land up on the hill had been given to somebody else. Well, I was speechless, and disgusted. We had travelled across the world to be told to go and repossess land for this woman? Never mind that all the land was ours in the first place, and we didn't get a brass razoo for it. The woman didn't even invite us into her house. Talk about Russian hospitality. Instead of arguing with this ignorant woman, we just turned around and walked away.

We went on, reaching the Douzhena bridge and the *Zarinok* — public land, which had hardly changed in our absence. Olga often grazed there, but she was more interested in the fabulous growth across the river, which was Government land.

Then further along lived the Hapaten family, but I had no idea which of them had survived the war. So I left Ruthie resting by the side of the road and proceeded further to find the Hapaten abode. I saw a man working in the fields, so I walked up to him and asked: "Do you know Hapaten?" He looked at me suspiciously. "Who wants to know?" he demanded. So I introduced myself, but he did not remember. However, I recognised him: it was Stefan Hapaten, and we had been bosom buddies in our younger days. So he took me to meet his family; Stefan already had grandchildren, and I was introduced to them all. Stefan poured a few glasses of vodka. But the house was shared with a multitude of flies, all buzzing around. Presently, the wife appeared with a plateful of steaming pork sausages, which I graciously refused, but the flies had no such compunction; they descended on the plate in a feeding frenzy. But Stefan still didn't remember me; however, he did recall a mutual friend named Yerichem.

Then, after three wholesome glasses of vodka and much more reminiscing, I had to make tracks. It seems that Stefan spent some years in Soviet prisons and now was in diminished health and living on a Russian pension. This was interesting stuff and I wanted to hear more, but Ruthie was down the street alone, and the hour was late, so I invited them all outside for a family picture, a few friendly hugs and some teary goodbyes.

Then I got back to Ruthie on her pile of rocks, and she wasn't at all happy.

"Why did you stay that long?" she demanded.

Well, a pile of rocks wasn't really the place to leave a loving wife, but she did not speak the language, and was hardly overjoyed that people were fussing over me and ignoring her. But she wasn't being ignored — it only appeared that way. I had a similar feeling in London, when Ruthie's family made a fuss of her and I was left in the lurch.

Anyway, it was already 6.00pm, so we began the tiresome journey back to town. The Douzhena bridge was there, in its full glory, and next to it was Reb Benzin's property. That piece of land used to get flooded every time it rained, but now it had a new house on it, and women were working in the distance. So, after talking to a neighbour, I found out that the property belonged to the Bozsenyuk family. Well, I used to know Marika Bozsenyuk, so I got very excited and knocked on the door. A giant of a man opened it, and after I told him who I was looking for, he said, "You are here to see my mother."

Then Marika appeared; her husband followed with all the little grand-children. Marika's two sisters, Olena and Anna, appeared, and soon we were asked inside to celebrate this auspicious occasion, with a few glasses of vodka. Well, we reminisced about the old times, and exchanged teary memories in the process. I used to know Marika as a child of five or six, and we did have fun times. Outside the house, I managed to take a few photographs, and was so pleased that we had re-established contact with another of my long lost contemporaries. I gave her my mother's address in Israel and she wrote to my mother a couple of times.

Tchorna Tisa had no electric light or any other mod cons, but it still oozed much character and charm. I somehow preferred our dark Tchorna Tisa to Jasina's electric pylons, with the little flickering lights that lit up the glaring poverty of the town. I would have loved to spend a week here and re-acquaint myself with the mountains and the *polo-ninas* — the high country, where the cattle went in the old days, and from which the milk was brought down on horseback once a week. I wish we could have explored the beautiful, undulating fields a great deal more.

I wanted to improve my Ruthenian dialect and establish a rapport with a few people, but it was not to be. However, we did see the snow-capped Hoverla Mountain in September, and this historic feature reminded me that some things never change.

Any people we greeted with a smile along the way certainly gave us a stealthy look — they seemed to suspect that we were deranged. But Ruthie persisted with her bravado, and soon our smiles melted even the iciest of Hutsul hearts; we were getting smiles back. So I began imagining that Ruthie would settle in Tchorna Tisa and become the toast of the town; but darkness was upon us, and we had to accelerate our pace. Ruth was leading the way and I followed, in a tired daze. My mind was still in Tchorna Tisa and I could hardly absorb it all.

Some 50 years of my life had passed since I had lived here, and with the passing of these years all we had possessed had gone. So the few fleeting hours we now had were certainly not enough to catch up on a lifetime.

Chapter 43

A stranger in my own town

I often marvel at the spectacular leaps humanity has made into the unknown since World War II. Today we have computers, robots, mechanised tractors, automated cars, coffee percolators, and even prospective trips into the celestial beyond. I really think that, had our forebears seen what was coming, they would have instantly retired to their graves.

The living standards of our 'civilised' existence in Tchorna Tisa 50 years ago have deteriorated while life in the west has moved forward in leaps and bounds. Zakarpatska Ukraina, or former Carpathia, has been left behind in the modern stakes. There, they still have their wooden outhouses, newspaper is still used as toilet paper, and the contents of the overflowing boxes are buried in the cabbage patches. Now the population may not have much entertainment, but the cabbages do thrive on the human excreta.

I suppose we had to have a good reserve of foolish enthusiasm and an abundance of outrageous tenacity, to return to Zakarpatska Ukraina. But returning to Tchorna Tisa in 1992 was a sobering experience.

The most distressing thing was that I felt a complete stranger in my own town. Nothing made any sense after an absence of 47 years. The Jews who used to live in the old houses had been massacred by the Nazis, and the new occupants were total strangers to us, and spoke

Russian dialects. They had destroyed all the goodwill and neighbourly cohesion there once had been.

Ruth and I gained the impression that Ukrainian independence had done nothing for the standard of living. In fact, scarcities were widespread and possibly avoidable. Fifty years ought to have been more than adequate to get most things back on track, yet bread rationing was still a daily chore. There was also a lively black market.

The Ukrainian women had become a different breed; they no longer wore their colourful embroideries and unique *zapaskes*. The *postole* with the long leather straps had also gone. I remembered the women's long shirts, all gathered up at the waist, which made a useful pouch for the necessities of life. Did the women now wear brassieres and panties? I should have asked about that. Similarly, in my younger days, they had had to make do with improvised colours for powder, rouge and lipstick. I wondered if this had changed, over 50 years. I also noticed that the men's embroidered shirts, riding breeches, sleeveless sheep-skins and the inevitable *postole*, with the colourful, woollen socks had also gone. The old-fashioned clothing was but a memory; its place was now monopolised by drab, ill-fitting garb — mostly home-made.

Oh, the proud Hutsuls of yesteryear had vanished almost without trace. Gone were their bright appearance and outlook. They worried about feeding their families. They used to be proud foresters and keen farmers, but their descendants did neither.

The rationing we experienced in Tchorna Tisa in 1992 took me back to the worst times of World War II, when the Jews were being starved, and grew lentils and maize and ate boiled grass to sustain themselves. These were the times when the strength to survive was at a premium; when the Nazis slaughtered the Jews in Auschwitz, Treblinka, Mauthausen and in hundreds of other places.

Well, what was wrong with the forests, the river streams and the whole Ukrainian economy? Why wasn't the world utilising the soft wood? In earlier years, the Hutsuls had prospered and even imported workers to labour in the forests.

I explained to Ruth how the old times had worked: how the forest was always the provider of employment and how people cherished the work in them. The forests had fallen silent. It seemed that the change-over from Podkarpatska Russ to Zakarpatska Ukraina had stifled all progress. Nobody wanted the Carpathian logs anymore.

Well, it all seemed a diabolic contradiction: Tchorna Tisa without its pine forests? Unheard of. But the new fashion was for the Ukrainian men to scour Europe for employment and let the forests grow to their heart's content while the women keep the farms going. The Ukrainian preoccupation was now to save up enough dough to get to the jobs in continental Europe. But once there, they found difficulties getting work. The Ukrainians had no special training, apart from picking fruit and repairing fences. There wasn't much going for untrained staff, unless they worked in factories. Even our landlord, Mishka Dominyuk (Natasha's husband), was away for most of the year, and took any job going in Germany or the Czech Republic.

Wouldn't you say that this Ukrainian independence has killed the golden goose? Oh, how the mighty have fallen …The times have certainly changed in Europe since Czechoslovakia disintegrated. It is not all that long ago that the Hutsul kids thought schooling was a waste of time; their prime ambition was forest work rather than education.

Even the Carpathian waterways have gone to ruin. I wonder what happens to all this the melting snow in the spring? I know that the rivers carry it away to the flat parts, but is anyone making use of it? In my time, the rivers and creeks use to flood, and carry away bridges and all else in their paths.

The old lumber-jacks, the viable timber industry and the colourful Hutsul garb, all had vanished. Well, thank G-d for the old Tchorna Tisa streets, the bridges and the Jewish cemetery — at least they all still looked familiar.

Eventually we got back to our lodgings in Jasina. Then after the evening meal our host, Mishka, invited us to join him in the market place, a routine that neither he nor the rest of the population ever missed. Mishka always met his cronies on the southern side of the bridge — a nightly, sacrosanct ritual, where they could reminisce, smoke a few cigarettes then return to their abodes. Life plodded along in Jasina, just as long as the men could congregate around the Iron Bridge.

Our stay in Jasina , which include visits to the cemetery and Tchorna Tisa, lasted several days. Then we started our journey back home. First stop was to collect our luggage from Ludmila's place, and then board a train for Bratislava, my birthplace.

There were a number of Gipsies sitting on the floor on the train, and another one joined them, saying: "My place is also on the floor." I couldn't understand this. They had train tickets like all other commuters, but still saw themselves as outcasts? The Gipsies were always treated as second class citizens — bowing and scraping to all and sundry, living in squalor. This was very much in evidence on our train, where the Gipsies were freely abused even as they were huddled on the floor. I sat there wondering: was this inherent or inculcated prejudice? And why did the Gipsies tolerate it? Was this prejudice a characteristic of Eastern Europe?

Before the war, the Jews were treated like that, but the State of Israel changed everything. Israel has rehabilitated the Jews, and given them credibility and pride of place in society. Even the Diaspora Jews have acquired an unprecedented status — but the poor Gipsies remain a race apart. On that train, did none of the travellers feel diminished because of the way they treated the poor Gipsies? One fat Hungarian even said: "The Gipsy's place is at our feet." In fact, the Hungarians call the Gipsies *Cigany* which encompasses all the unsavoury adjectives of the Teutonic language. As a Holocaust Survivor, I cannot tolerate it. These attitudes must be combated, otherwise history will repeat itself.

Arriving in Bratislava for a quick look around, it appeared to be just another provincial town, hardly the capital of an independent state. In fact, the whole of Slovakia was experiencing an economic downturn, and the shops certainly reflected this state of affairs. Anyway, Ruth and I were pleased to leave these stagnant economies and head for greener pastures.

Prague presented a refreshing change of scenery, and we entered a totally civilised world. All the stores were well stocked and there was no shortage of anything; even the people in the streets were unspoiled by Communism. We found them very friendly and outgoing — a striking difference between Slovakia and Zakarpatska Ukraina. In 1992 I recalled the warmth, the friendship and the hospitality we had received from the people of Prague on our return from the camps some 50 years earlier.

Chapter 44

Return to the classroom

Now in retirement, I have cut down on my activities and applied all the zeal at my disposal to chasing an inscrutable ball on the golf course. This is a hobby I did not acquire in Tchorna Tisa or, for that matter, in Sydney. However, the staff of the department of radiology at Prince of Wales Hospital made my decision for me; they presented me with a full set of golf clubs on my retirement.

After lingering in professional limbo for a while I returned to the classroom to study autobiographical writing. I felt I had survived so I could attest to the atrocities half a century earlier. As well as delving into my long life story I had a message to young people of today—the Holocaust is not a unique occurrence—it was perpetrated by people really not very different from us. Bad times produce bad people, and bad people produce holocausts, and it can happen again. Lest we forget.

I began to encourage other survivors to tell their stories, just as I was doing. Soon I was formally teaching autobiographical writing two nights per week at Eastern Suburbs Evening College and Randwick College. Not just with survivors but with students of all ages and all walks of life. At the end of each term I always asked my students to evaluate the class and give me written feedback. I was always humbled to hear their kind words as to how I had helped them get their personal stories out of their hearts and on to paper. Six years of teaching has been a very rewarding experience for both the ageing pupils and their budding teacher. Little did I know that I would have such an impact on my students and their families[10].

The proud moment after receiving The Order of Australia Medal.
Peter, Bonita, Ruth and Albert, May, 1983, Government House, Sydney.

---

10   In late 1998 seeing that he was having increasing difficulties in the classroom, he voluntarily retired.

Afterword

In 1999 Albert was diagnosed with Alzheimer's and over the next thirteen or so years we watched how this awful disease slowly robbed us of the father we once knew. However, unlike the experiences of other sufferers who created turmoil for their loved ones, with erratic and often disturbing behaviour, our Dad's decline was a relatively peaceful journey. As the disease progressed it etched away the guarded exterior we knew from our childhood and revealed what we believed to be the true essence of our dad. He smiled more and became more openly affectionate, showering his loved ones with kisses and hugs.

Our Mum was his primary carer for the first seven years, as we were living in the United States. In 2007 he was fortunate enough to be one of the first residents in the Special Care Unit of the Randwick Montefiore Home. He remained there, dignified and gentle until the very end. In January 2013 he was buried at Rookwood Jewish Cemetery in Sydney.

It was his honesty and integrity that set him apart, and what he tried to instill in us. He was a compassionate man, a kind soul, a humanitarian, a teacher and mentor to so many people. The small skinny kid from Tchorna Tisa left an indelible mark on all of us.

Peter and Bonita Halm

May, 2016

Appendix

SURVIVORS of the SHOAH
VISUAL HISTORY FOUNDATION

8 December 1995

Albert Halm
████████████
████████████████
Australia

Dear Mr. Halm,

In sharing your personal testimony as a survivor of the Holocaust, you have granted future generations the opportunity to experience a personal connection with history.

Your interview will be carefully preserved as an important part of the most comprehensive library of testimonies ever collected. Far into the future, people will be able to see a face, hear a voice, and observe a life, so that they may listen and learn, and always remember.

Thank you for your invaluable contribution, your strength, and your generosity of spirit.

All my best,

Steven Spielberg
Chairman

June 5, 1977.

Dr. Joseph Kermish,
Head - Archives Division,
Yad Vashem,
JERUSALEM.

Dear Dr. Kermish,

You may recall my recent visit to your office when I handed you a wooden box
containing some 1,400 names and other details of victims from Ebensee, Austria.
At the time you requested a statement from me, but I was unable to supply it
en route; I was attending various congresses. However, now that I have returned home I still do not know what a statement issued over thirty years later should contain, but I do appreciate that you need some reference to the
events.

May I point out that this important information was not withheld for thirty-
two years, it was communicated in detail to an Agency of the United Nations
and to the World Jewish Congress in 1945. However, I promised myself at the
concentration camp that if I am spared and we are blessed with a Jewish State
I shall personally deposit the information in Martyrs' Memorial in Jerusalem.
In 1973 I attempted the pilgrimage, but was not permited to board the plane
in Rome due to the Yom Kippur war. In 1977 I succeeded in delivering the file
and was privileged to see a most fitting memorial to all who perished so need-
lessly. Words fail me to describe my emotions, but my ambition is now full-
filled.

I was 18 years of age when taken from Podkarpatska Russ by the Germans in
1944 to Auschwitz, Mauthausen and Ebensee. In Ebensee I developed an infectious illness and was placed in the Infectious Block which later became the
hospital for Jews. The hospital was adjacent to the Crematorium and was a
factory of death, the infectious cases were no longer segregated and six
patients were generally allocated to each bunk. Each patient had his name, date
of birth and the diagnosis written on a slip of paper on the bunk-head. I was
given a cleaning job in the hospital and this enabled me to move around and
remove the slips of paper as soon as patients passed away. The pieces of paper
were carefully secreted in rags under the building and were often in danger of
being discovered by dogs. This activity went on for 14 months till the Camp
was liberated by the Americans. In that time I was able to keep a record of
every death in the hospital and was almost discovered a mere two hours before
the liberating army marched into the Camp.

The file contains only Jewish victims who died in the hospital; the hundreds
of thousands who perished outside in the camp are unaccounted. Each slip of
paper has a cross and a date in red which signifies the date of death. Often
there is other information: time of death, place of origin, occupation, number
of children, wife's name, etc. This information was obtained from other inmates
who knew the victims. The letters which precede each serial number signify
the nationality i.e. "U.J." Ungarischer Jude, "D.J." Deutscher Jude, etc.
The diagnoses were often false and fictitious as were the causes of deaths.
The information obtained was often scribbled on the slip of paper in the language in which it was given and I hope the deciphering does not prove too difficult, should it ever be necessary.

This is about as much as I can remember of the events, but should you have any
queries please do not hesitate to write to me. Dr. Kermish, I was exceedingly
pleased to have met you and hope we shall meet again. I wish you strength and
perseverance in your noble task. With kindest regards,

YAD VASHEM
MARTYRS' AND HEROES'
REMEMBRANCE AUTHORITY
JERUSALEM

יד ושם
רשות הזיכרון
לשואה ולגבורה
ירושלים

Jerusalem, July 19, 1977

Mr. Albert Halm
▓▓▓▓▓▓▓▓▓▓▓▓▓▓
▓▓▓▓▓▓▓▓▓▓▓▓▓▓▓▓▓▓▓▓

Dear Mr. Halm,

Thank you very much for the wooden box with 1,400 Ebensee cards
and your letter of June 5, concerning their origin. We particularly
appreciate the fact that you took it upon yourself to bring this
collection to us in person.

We noted that at age 18 you were taken from Podkarpatska Russ to
Auschwitz, Mauthausen and finally Ebensee. After been taken ill
you were brought to the Jewish hospital, the Infectious Block at
Ebensee. This hospital which was next to the Crematorium was in
fact a death factory since the infectious patients were no longer
segregated and they soon died. Six patients were generally allocated to each bunk. Each patient had his name, date of birth and
the diagnosis written on a slip of paper on the bunk head. You were
given the job of cleaning the hospital and while carrying out your
task you were able to remove the slips of paper from the bunk heads
of the dead and thus gather a most valuable information file, which
you hid, wrapped in rags under the building. We have also noted
that you took upon yourself to gather information on the deceased,
collecting the details from their friends. All this, for a period
of 14 months and were almost found out just two hours before the
liberation of the camp.

We greatly appreciate your most valuable collection of the Ebensee
files which you presented to our Archives and we have noted the
very maticulous way in which you gathered, under most perilous
conditions, the slips of paper the remnant of those of our people
who perished in Ebensee.

These memorial files will be kept in our Archives and will serve in
addition to enlighten students and scholars of the Holocaust.

Please note that the files appear in our Archives entrance book
under registry 4474.

Sincerely yours,

Dr. J. Kermisz,

BACKGROUND INFORMATION (ALBERT HALM, FIR, JP, OAM)

Involved in underground activities as a teenager in Czechoslovakia during
WW2. Interned and sent to Auschwitz andwhence to several other concentration camps until liberated by the American forces in Ebensee, Austria.
Upon return to Prague recuperated then was employed by an organization
which was responsible for returning property to the Jews previously confiscated by the Germans.

In 1947 left Prague under the auspices of the American HIAS and the
Australian Jewish Welfare Society to settle in Australia. After learning
English for a time, enrolled into a Radio Trades Course and served a
5 year apprenticeship. Worked as a tradesman for two years then undertook
a 2 year course in medical radiography and joined Sydney Hospital as
a student radiographer. After qualifying was appointed radiographer at
Prince of Wales Hospital, where remained for 27 years and still current-
ly employed as Chief Radiographer.

In that time was involved in numerous research projects and regularly
contributed to national and international professional journals and
technical conferences. He was a speaker at the 5th and 7th World Congress
of the International Society of Radiographers in Madrid and Brussels and
at the 2nd Regional Conference of the Americas in Kingston, Jamaica.
He also delivered papers at the 4th World Congress of the International
Radiation Protection Society in Paris and at the 10th National Conference
of American Hospital Radiology Administrators in Las Vegas. He was also
the 17th James N. Young Memorial Orator of the Australian Institute of
Radiography and twice winner of the Medical Applications Award for out-
outstanding technico-clinical papers.
He has been a part-time teacher and examiner at the Sydney Technical
College for 12 years. He is now a specialist lecturer in radiography,
a Fellow of the Australian Institute of Radiography and a member of
its Fellowship Evaluation Panel. He is also a member of the Radiography
Course Advisory Committee of the Department of Technical and Further
Education and a former member of the Federal Management Committee of
the Australian Radiation Protection Society.

He is the current chairman of the Chief Administrative
Radiographers Group and former chairman of the Radiation Protection
Committee and member of the Ethics Committee of the Australian Insti-
tute of Radiography.

He also works for various social and charitable causes and is a former
member of the Association for Mental Health an associate member of
the Medical Association for Prevention of War and Immediate Past-president
of the Kingsford Maroubra Hebrew Congregation. He is the current chairman of the Association of Jewish Holocaust Survivors (N.S.W.).

YEAR	ORGANISATION	POSITION HELD
48 - 53	Radio Centre P/Ltd	Apprentice, Radio Trades
53 - 54	" "	Radio Technician
54 - 56	Sydney Hospital	Student in Radiography
56 - 58	" "	Radiographer
58 - 82	Prince of Wales Hospital	Chief Radiographer
68 - 76	Sydney Technical College	Part-time Teacher
76 - 82	" " "	Part-time Senior Lecturer
65 - 82	Australian Institute of Radiography	Fellow
79 - 82	Department of Technical and Further Education	Member Radiography Course Advisory Committee
79 - 81	Australian Radiation Protection S'ty	Member - Federal Management Committee
80 - 82	Australian Institute of Radiography	Member - Fellowship Evaluation Panel
1967	Australian Institute of Radiography	17th James N. Young Memorial Orator
1967	" " "	Winner - Medical Applications Award
1971	" " "	Winner - " " "
1973	International Society of Radiographers & Radiol. Tech.	Speaker - 5th World Congress, Madrid
1977	International Radiation Protection Society	Speaker - 4th World Congress, Paris
1981	International Society of Radiographers & Radiol. Tech.	Speaker - 7th World Congress, Brussels
1982	American Hospital Radiology Administrators	Speaker - 10th National Congress, Las Vegas
1982	International Society of Radiographers & Radiol. Tech.	Speaker - 2nd Regional Congress, Kingston
54 - 68	N.S.W. Jewish Board of Deputies	Deputy
68 - 78	Kingsford-Maroubra Congregation	Executive Member & Vice-President
78 - 82	" " "	President

Curriculum Vitae   Albert Halm

POSITIONS HELD

1960 to 1990 - Manager of the Department of Diagnostic Radiology and
              Chief Radiographer, Prince of Wales Hospital, Sydney.

1968 to 1989 - Specialist Part-time Lecturer in Radiography, Technical and Further Education.

1978 to 1987 - Examiner, Radiography Course, Technical and Further Education.

1980 to 1985 - Member of Radiography Course Advisory Committee, Technical and
              Further Education.

1980 to 1985 - Chairman, Chief Administrative Radiographers, Universities' Teaching
              Hospitals of New South Wales.

1981 to 1984 - Member, Management Committee, Australian Radiation Protection Society .

1983 to 1987 - Examiner, Fellowship Evaluation Panel, Australian Institute of Radiography.

    1987 -   Member, MRT Evaluation Com'tee, Newcastle College of Advanced Education.

1988 to 1993 - Specialist Lecturer and Examiner (part-time), Medical Radiation Technology,
              Cumberland College of Health Sciences, Sydney University.

SUMMARY OF CLINICO-TECHNICAL PUBLICATIONS

    "Plastic Adhesives for Bonding Fractures" - USA

    "Modern Radiographic Procedures in the Demonstration of Hodgkin's Disease" - USA

    "Calcific and Sclerotic Landmarks in Radiography" - UK

    "Radiography in Hepato-Biliary Diagnosis" - UK

    "Lymphography and Supplementary Procedures" - UK

    "Risk-Benefit Discrepancies in Radiodiagnostic Medicine" - France

    "Dramatic Results in Biliary Radiography" - Australia

    "Casualties in a Sophisticated Society" - Australia

    "Specialised Radiography in the Malformed and Diseased Spine" - Australia

CLINICO-TECHNICAL PUBLICATIONS Continued

"How Elusive is the Double Gall-Bladder" - Australia

"Important Refinements in Lymphangiography" - Australia

"An Autobiography of a 14 x 17" Film" - Australia

"Indelible Landmarks in Radiography" - Australia

"Radiation Abuse and Its Effects" - Australia

"Intra-Medullary Splinting" - Australia

INVITED SPEAKER TO INTERNATIONAL CLINICO-TECHNICAL CONFERENCES

Madrid - Spain - 1973	Brussels - Belgium - 1981	Las Vegas - USA - 1982
Paris - France - 1977	Kingston - Jamaica - 1982	London - UK - 1986

RECOGNITION AND AWARDS

1965 - Fellowship Award, Australian Institute of Radiography

1967 - The NSW James N Young Orator, Australian Institute of Radiography

1967 - Annual Award for Best Technico-Clinical Paper Presented at National Technical Conference in Brisbane

1971 - Annual Award for Best Technico-Clinical Paper Presented at National Technical Conference in Melbourne

1983 - Order of Australia Medal (OAM) for Medicine Especially Radiography

* Chairman, Chief Administrative Radiographers' Group, of the New South Wales University Teaching Hospitals.

* Former Member, Ethical Sub-committee of the Australian Institute of Radiography.

* Former Member, Evaluation Committee of the Newcastle College of Advanced Education - Diploma of Applied Science in Medical Radiation Technology for the NSW Higher Education Board.

EDUCATIONAL ACTIVITIES

* James N Young Memorial Orator - Sydney.

* Invited Speaker at the 5th, 7th and 8th World Congress of the International Society of Radiographers held respectively in Madrid (Spain), Brussels (Belgium) and Kingston (Jamaica).
* Invited Speaker to 4th World Congress of the International Radiation Protection Society, held in Paris (France).
* Invited Speaker to the 10th National Congress of the American Hospital Radiology Administrators, held in Las Vegas - USA.
* Former presenter of many papers at the Annual National Technical Conferences of the Australian Institute of Radiography.
* Former Lecturer and Facilitator in the Art of Diagnostic Radiography at a variety of public fora.
* Now, Lecturer and Facilitator in Autobiographical Writing with the Eastern Suburbs Regional Evening College - Sydney.

AWARDS

Fellowship of the Australian Institute of Radiography

Recipient of the Medical Applications Award (Twice) for Scientific Papers

Order of Australia Medal for Work in Medicine especially Radiography.

AREA OF ABIDING INTEREST

Abusive practices in Facilitating Diagnostic Radiation Services.

Greater educational emphasis on the harmful affects of Diagnostic Radiation.

* * * *

MY CONTRIBUTION TO THE GENERAL INSURANCE CLAIMS REVIEW PANEL: Will be in the area of expertise in judging the possible excessive exposures to diagnostic radiation in today's modern society. I might add that Radiation Safety has always been my primary professional concern during the 35 years of engagement.

Nelly (1905-1997) and Albert (1925-2013)

CPSIA information can be obtained
at www.ICGtesting.com
Printed in the USA
LVOW03s1502110617
537725LV00034B/1700/P

9 780648 015406